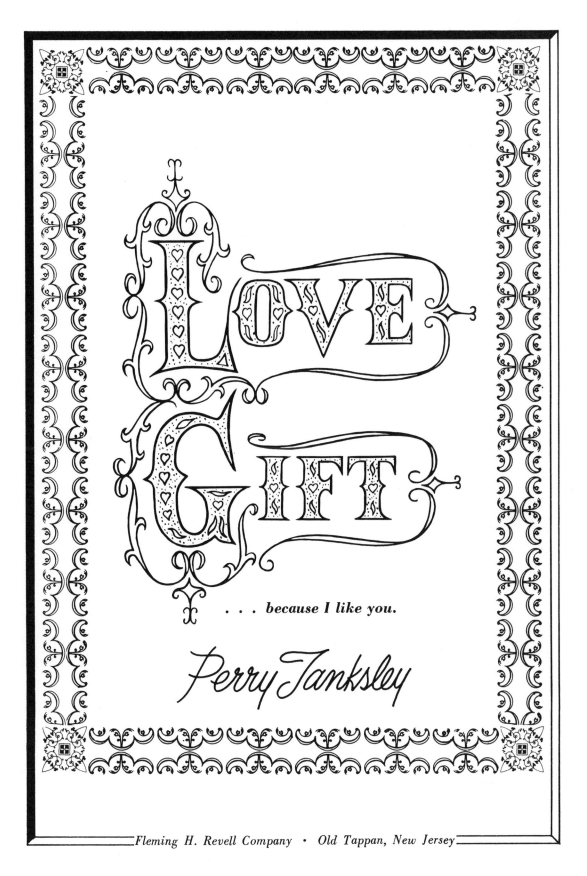

LOVE GIFT

. . . *because I like you.*

Perry Tanksley

Fleming H. Revell Company · Old Tappan, New Jersey

Scripture quotations are from the *Revised Standard Version of the Bible,* Copyrighted 1946 and 1952.

Diligent effort has been made to credit the authors of all quoted material.

The poems in this volume were written by Perry Tanksley.

Contents

...because I like you.

or He has said, "I will never fail you nor forsake you."
Hebrews 13:5

THE VISITOR

For years each day at six A.M.
He went to church and bowed his knee
And meekly prayed, "Dear God, it's Jim."
And when he'd leave we all could see
The Presence came and walked with him.
As Jim grew old the chastening rod
Of years left him so ill and drawn
His path to church is now untrod;
But in his room each day at dawn
He hears a voice, "Dear Jim, it's God!"

Jesus said, "Lo, I am with you always, to the close of the age." **Matthew 28:20**

Accepting Adversity

God had one Son on earth without sin, but never one without suffering.   Saint Augustine

I MET GOD IN DEPTH

I met God in the path
Of carefree youthful days,
And in the business rush
Of feverish prosperous ways.
I met Him in the midst
Of seeking fame and wealth,
And at an altar place
And in the bloom of health.
But I, in looking back,
Am sure I did not know
My Lord in truest sense
'Till illness brought me low.
'Twas then I learned to trust
In Christ the Lord alone,
And illness showed me God
In ways I'd never known.
I'd known in casual ways
My Lord across the years,
But I met Him in depth
Through illness and through tears.

What a debt the world owes the sufferers! Progress in every field of endeavor may be credited directly or indirectly to that army of undecorated heroes, the patient sufferers.

I have known more of God since I came to this bed than through all my life.

—Ralph Erskine

Despise not thy school of sorrow, O my Soul; it will give thee a unique part in the universal song.   —George Matheson

The brightest crowns that are worn in heaven have been tried, and smelted, and polished, and glorified through the furnace of tribulation.
                    —Edwin Hubbell Chapin

UNCONFINED

Some say I am confined to bed
But I don't think they know
That though my body is shut in
I still am on the go.
I go to visit those I love
And walk to market place;
I tread the woods until it rains
And then the rainbow trace.
Of course my body cannot go
For it's been ill for days,
But who would say a room confines
A soul and mind that prays?
Although my body is shut in
Through days of darkest night,
My spirit soars on wings of prayer
And moves with speed of light.
In prayer I visit those I love;
Great is the gift of prayer;
And when my thoughts are beamed toward you
You'll sense my presence there.

Rejoice in your hope, be patient in tribulation.
Romans 12:12

Achievement and Ambition

**Get your happiness out of your work or you will
never know what happiness is.**

EACH LEAVES HIS OWN MEMORIAL

Sir Christopher Wren, astronomer,
Left his vocational standing
And launched at forty-eight, a life
Of architectural planning.
At eighty-nine he died content,
A celebrated man,
For fifty-three cathedrals stood
Which he himself had planned.
With plaques and stones friends honored him
Until an editorial
Said, "Look around! With life and deeds
He built his own memorial."
'Twas then I saw, each with kind deeds
Or else of stones bequeath
Some lovely thing—a poem, a church,
Or else of love a wreath.

You will never be saved by works, but let us
tell you most solemnly that you will never be
saved without works.　　　—Theodore Cuyler

To get a job done, give it to a busy man. He'll
get his secretary to do it.

It is two percent genius and ninety-eight percent
honest effort that brings about success in any
line of work.　　　　　　—Thomas A. Edison

Remember when they didn't have to use "Men
Working" signs. You could tell they were work-
ing by watching them.　　　—Tode Tuttle

If I have done any deed worthy of remembrance,
that deed will be my monument. If not, no
monument can preserve my memory.
　　　　　　　　　　　　　　—Agesilaus

MY SOUL POSSESSES WINGS

Dear Lord, don't let me be
Content with little things;
My mind has thought great thoughts;
My soul possesses wings.
Dear Lord, I will not be
Content with little thoughts,
For I have had a glimpse
Of deeds which great men wrought.
Dear Lord, I cannot be
Content with little dreams,
For I have daring plans;
My soul possesses wings.
Dear Lord, lest I should be
Content with little deeds,
Let my exploits expand
Untried and time-worn creeds.

**In quietness and in trust shall be your strength.
Isaiah 30:15**

Aging Attractively

There is nothing more beautiful than cheerfulness in an old face.   **Jean Paul Richter**

THE GOLDEN YEARS

I know why latter years
Are called the golden years;
Gold is a precious gift
Wherever it appears.
Gold is a treasure rare
Which none would dare deny
Growing in elegance
As years go swiftly by.
So latter years of life
Are golden years that shine
With worth that makes me proud
Of every one of mine.

Some hearts, like evening primroses, open more beautifully in the shadows of life.

I have attained my seventy-fifth birthday. You must not wonder at me even at seventy-five, eager to remain here in the high place of the missionary field, for opportunities of service were never greater and the out-look for a great harvest never brighter than now.
—Missionary Hudson Taylor writing from China.

DECEMBER YEARS

Let me grow older, Lord,
Thinking thoughts of beauty
And doing golden deeds
Beyond the call of duty.
And let me spread sunshine
For there is so much room
For people sharing gladness
Instead of spreading gloom.
And as I daily age,
Lord, let faith conquer fears
That zest for living life
May crown December years.

SO CHERISH UNLIVED YEARS

There's not one time in life
When all is good or bad,
For life's a blending of
The joyful and the sad.
And every phase of life
Repays in its own way,
And brings us joy enough
To brighten every day.
So cherish unlived years—
Tomorrow's path untrod—
Assured they're fragments of
The perfect will of God.

My times are in thy hand.   **Psalms 31:15**

Answer to Atheism

An atheist cannot find God for the same reason a thief cannot find a policeman.

Atheists and agnostics pray when they see no other way out of their troubles.

CAN ONE VIEW CREATION?

How can one look at stars,
Or tread a tree-fringed sod,
Or hear birds sing at dawn
And say there is no God?
How can one scan the sea,
Or ride an ocean breaker,
Or view a far-off mountain
And swear there is no Maker?
How can one view creation
And not feel like a traitor
While arrogantly insisting
There is no Creator?

HE'S LEFT FOOTPRINTS

God made this universe
And none of us can grasp
How stars were sprayed through space.
Oh, what a wondrous task!
He scooped the valleys out
And stacked the mountains up,
And tacked His carpet green
With fragrant buttercups.
And He's left footprints here
On sky and sea and sod,
And only men born blind
Can say there is no God.

HE'S REAL TO ME

I've never heard His voice
Nor glimpsed His face so wise
Or gripped His nail-torn hand
Or gazed into His eyes.
Yet echoes of His voice
I've heard above the storm
And oft at worship time
I've glimpsed His shadowed form.
His robe I've never touched
Or heard Him call my name,
Yet He's more real to me
Than any friend I claim.

YOU HAVE A RIGHT TO DOUBT

You have a right to doubt
The deeds on sacred page
'Til Christ in you has wrought
The miracle of the age.
I knew He calmed the storm
And marched upon the sea
When He first hushed my fears
And came to walk with me.
I doubt no more He spoke
And water blushed to wine,
Since my stained heart He changed
Into His snow-white shrine.

Orthodoxy of words is atheism unless backed up by excellent character.

May we shout for joy over your victory, and in the name of our God set up our banners!

Psalms 20:5

Art of Appreciation

The deepest principle of human nature is the craving to be appreciated. **William James**

If you want to live more you must master the art of appreciating the little, everyday blessings of life. This is not altogether a golden world, but there are countless gleams of gold to be discovered in it if we give our minds to them.
—Henry Alford Porter

The little letters we write to friends, the clusters of flowers with which we enrich their lives, the almost insignificant acts of kindness and love, these are the treasures we lay up to warm our hearts with when old age creeps in and beckons youth away. —Thomas Drier

PROUD TO STAND BY HIM

The preacher urged his church
When all his words were through,
"Go stand by some aged friend
Who's meant the most to you."
They passed the rich and great
As many took their stand
By one who seldom spoke,
An obscure older man.
But he in winsome ways
Had shared his faith with them,
And they in gratitude
Were proud to stand by him.

UNCRIPPLED MIND

A little boy at Christmas time
Had legs all braced with steel,
But learned to use his crutches well
And one might say with skill.
He joined the crowd on Christmas morn
Who trod the path to church,
And he attached a holly wreath
Onto each sturdy crutch.
He tied some tiny Christmas bells
Onto each metal brace
And cried, "God bless us all," as smiles
Were wreathed upon his face.
"How can you smile?" One asked. He said,
"The braces that I wear
Are on my legs, but not my mind,
For I'm not crippled there."
"And though my legs are lame," he said,
"For life I have a plan;
I'll give my best and hope to get
All out of life I can!"

He too serves a certain purpose who only stands and cheers. —Henry Adams

It is not what happens to you, but the way you take it that counts. —Hilys Jasper

Lead a life worthy of God, who calls you into his own kingdom and glory. **1 Thessalonians 2:12**

Bearing Burdens

The best helping hand is found at the end of your own arm.

WHEN THE CHURCH PRAYS

A burden lifted from his heart,
A load he could not bear,
Yet he knew not back home his church
Was remembering him in prayer.
She sensed the uplift hope inspires,
And strong faith made her merry,
But she knew not her church was praying
For her, its missionary.
Grief-stricken by his first-born's grave,
He heard the Master saying,
"Be strong!"—But he knew not back home
His church for him was praying.
When dark clouds lift and light breaks through
We're usually unaware
That someone back home who loves us
Has called our name in prayer.

IF I HAD KNOWN

If I had only known
The burden that you bore
I would have taken time
To knock upon your door,
Or I'd have cheered you up
When on a busy street
Your path and mine today
Did accidentally meet.
Tonight I'm sad for words
I was too dumb to say
When you had such a need
And I was blind today.

There is no exercise better for the heart than reaching down and lifting people up.

—John Holmer

There are two ways of exerting one's strength: one is pushing down, the other is pulling up.

—Booker T. Washington

AWKWARD CROSS-BEARING

When Christ bestows His cross
It is a sign I'd say
He's giving us a chance
To bless His world today.
And I think all cross-bearers
Help or hinder Christ's cause,
For crosses awkward-borne
May make some trip and fall.
Then let's beware lest we
Bear awkwardly our cross,
Or go complainingly
And cause souls to be lost.
Then let's so gladly bear
The cross our Lord entrusts,
That pilgrims travelling near
Will take heart knowing us.

Only a burdened heart can lead to fruitful service.

—Alan Redpath

Bear one another's burdens, and so fulfil the law of Christ. **Galatians 6:2**

Becoming Brotherly

God evidently does not intend us all to be rich, or powerful or great, but He does intend us all to be friends. **Ralph Waldo Emerson**

I ROSE TO BROTHER ALL

When I once prayed, "Our Father,"
My tears I could not hide.
That day, for the first time
I saw what it implied.
In theory I'd known all
Were sons of God above,
But I saw clearly then
We're brothers born of love.
I then began to live
By faith I'd long professed
And rose to brother all
Whom Jesus died to bless.

It's good to be our brother's keeper. It's better to be our brother's brother.

EARTH MUST CHOOSE BROTHERHOOD

Hats off to modern science
And scientists wise and good,
For through their skill the world
Became a neighborhood.
Science made the far-off lands
Seem like they're at our door,
And means of travel soon
Will shrink the world much more.
Science made a neighborhood;
One choice confronts us still:
Earth must choose brotherhood
Or be a battlefield.

That best portion of a good man's life, is his little, nameless, unremembered, acts of kindness and of love. —William Wordsworth

MY BROTHER

A beggar begged for bread
One summer evening time
And said to one well dressed,
"Could you lend me a dime?"
The business man turned all
His pockets inside out
And said, "My brother, I'm
As broke as you, no doubt!"
The beggar said, "The gift
You gave will go much further,
For I'm not hungry now
Since you called me your brother."

WISE INVESTMENT

You only gave a smile
Which cost you not a thing,
And yet it made me rich
As any ancient king.
You only gave a smile;
My name you did not call,
And yet it made my day
The brightest one of all.
But smiles elicit smiles.
And we each won a friend;
For something free, I'd say,
That's quite a dividend.

Let brotherly love continue. Do not neglect to show hospitality to strangers. **Hebrews 13:1-2**

Beholding Beauty

If you wisely invest in beauty it will remain with you through life.   **Frank Lloyd Wright**

HE JUNKS EACH MASTERPIECE

The Master-Artist paints
His world with brightest hue,
And then He switches scenes
Four times each year for you.
He first paints wintertime,
Contrasting black and white,
And yet on that drab scene
He beams his softest light.
Green is his favorite hue
For spring and summer scenes
And even orange-streaked fall
Is etched with evergreens.
But He loves flowers best
And stoops to paint them all
In colors that accent
Gay summer, spring and fall.
The Master-Artist paints
Nor ever fears to use,
Extravagance enough
To mix a hundred hues.
I think God loves to paint
For at the season's end
He junks each masterpiece
And slowly starts again.

Never lose an opportunity to see anything beauti-
ful. Beauty is God's handwriting.
—Charles Kingsley

STARVING FOR ROSES

Lord, we appreciate
The daily bread you give,
But now we know it takes
Much more than bread to live.
For life is difficult
With duty it imposes
And though we crave the bread,
We're starving for some roses.
In other words, dear Lord,
Let love enhance each duty
And life blend with romance;
And with our bread, give beauty.

WHAT IS BEAUTY?

I have a friend so young
With handsome face and fair
And there's an elegance
About her golden hair.
I have another friend
Who's lost her youthful grace,
For she's let hands of time
Pinch wrinkles in her face.
But rarer beauty dwells
With her whose hair is streaked,
For I see patience there
And love in wrinkled cheeks.

**He has made everything beautiful in its time;
also he has put eternity into man's mind.**
Ecclesiastes 3:11

Being Brave

Bravery is not the absence of fear, but the mastery of it.

A DOUBLE DOSE OF COURAGE

It startled me at first!
Yet by a mountain stream
I saw a blind man painting
A golden sunset scene.
At first I stood amazed,
Yet one with fingers gone
Was strumming his guitar
And humming low a song.
It seemed incredible!
Yet one who lost her child
Stood up in praise of God
And through her tears she smiled.
"Impossible," I said.
Yet sipping sorrow's cup
I saw a widow go
To cheer her neighbors up.
I doubted it at first,
Yet going to his store
My wheelchair neighbor smiled
Each day he passed my door.
How grand that God pours out
On those crushed down with sadness
A double dose of courage,
An extra cup of gladness.

A hero is no braver than an ordinary man, but he is brave five minutes longer.

COURAGEOUS MEN

This day demands courageous men
Who dauntless fight each evil trend.
Who dare to stand and speak for truth
Unfearful of harsh foes uncouth.
Men who affirm with bold reply,
"There are some things worse than to die."
Men who choose death on freedom's ground
Rather than live enslaved and bound.

Life is meant to be a heroic thing. God's best gift to His greatest servants has not been immunity from suffering or death but heroic faith and uttermost trust.   —George A. Gordon

ONE DAY AT A TIME

I know I cannot bear
The troubles of today
With fears of future years
And guilts of yesterday.
But God does not require
That I face present years
While burdened with past sins
And crushed with future fears.
But I can live today
And make it seem sublime
By learning how to live
Just one day at a time.

Behold, I have refined you, but not like silver; I have tried you in the furnace of affliction.

Isaiah 48:10

Believer's Blessings

Faith is to the soul what a mainspring is to a watch.

Don't stop with counting your blessings; think also of the misfortunes which you may have had but didn't.

I WONDER WHY THEY'RE SECRETS

Three secrets long concealed
Teach us we each can know
The secrets of spiritual living
And how we each can grow.
First, early every morn
Before the rush begins,
We must seek God in prayer.
Prayer lets God's love flow in.
Second, we must memorize
Before the day's half through
At least one verse of Scripture.
God's Word keeps Christians true.
Third, to grow as Christians
We'll find no better way
Than sharing Christ by witnessing
To one friend every day.
Doing such simple things
Each day and not infrequent,
Are secrets so transforming,
I wonder why they're secrets.

The Christian faith does not consist in belief that we are saved, but in the belief that we are loved.

THE OVERFLOW

Once God so filled me,
Such abundance I could not stand,
So I prayed impulsively,
"Dear God, withhold Thy hand!"
A thousand times
I've wished I could recall that hour
And feel again the Presence,
And sense the Spirit's power.
I'd pray, "Enlarge me, Lord,
And let Thy blessings pour,"
But most of all I'd pray,
"Dear God, let me run o'er."

NO JOY REQUIRED

An ecstasy of joy
By Christians oft is craved,
But feelings strong and joyful
Don't prove a person's saved.
God only asks we trust
The truth of every verse
Concerning Jesus Christ
And that He died for us.
For our emotions rise
And fall like window shades
While faith in Truth remains,
Unchanged and unafraid.
Christ taught a simple faith
Small as a mustard seed
Is all the Father asks
And all a person needs.

And without faith it is impossible to please him.
Hebrews 11:6

Character and Commitment

To climb higher, remain on the level.

DON'T DO AS ROMANS DO

If you should go to Rome
Don't do as Romans do
But act as they should act
Though many laugh at you.
Conduct yourself in Rome
As Romans ought to act
And they'll admire your stand
And some will change, in fact.
God's Kingdom only comes
When we at school and home
Act not as Romans do
But as they ought in Rome.

A man's character is like a fence—all the white-
wash in the world won't strengthen it.

A SERGEANT SPEAKS

A lad in my platoon
Would kneel each night and pray,
And boots we tossed at him
Were by our bunks next day.
He'd shine and place them there
When none of us could see,
And I saw Christ in him,
Through deeds he did for me.
He led me to the Lord,
And saved some rough recruits,
When he conveyed his faith
By shining muddy boots.

BY THIS YOU'RE BOUND

You are not bound to win each game
But you are bound to be
The kind of soul who leaves the field
Head high and conscience-free.
You are not bound to earn each game
The victor's golden crown,
But in defeat you must stand tall;
By this you're always bound.
And you're not bound to win if it
Means win at any cost,
But you are bound to keep the rules
Though every game is lost.
Nor are you bound to win at all
If in the victory earned,
Your self-respect and honor leave
To nevermore return.

PEOPLE KNOW!

Within a little town
A congregation heard
A fine evangelist
Proclaiming God's good Word.
While there, the preacher met
A godly man named Jim
And when the preacher left
He wrote a card to him.
Jim's last name was unknown
So on the card he wrote:
"To Jim, who walks with God,"
And Jim received that note.

*We rejoice in our sufferings, knowing that suffer-
ing produces endurance, and endurance produces
character, and character produces hope.*
Romans 5:3–4

o not delay me, since the Lord has prospered my way.
Genesis 24:56

WAIT LORD

"Thy kingdom come," I prayed
When our small prayer-group met,
But friends knew not I meant,
"Thy kingdom come, but not yet."
"Thy will be done," I prayed
Kneeling beside my mate,
But she knew not I meant,
"Thy will be done, but wait."
"Please use me, Lord," I prayed
When called upon to pray
But class-members knew not
I meant, "Use me, someday."
"Now bless me, Lord," I prayed
While I at church did bow,
And none knew God told me,
"I'll bless you, but not now."

*O Lord, hear; O Lord, forgive; O Lord, give heed
and act; delay not, for thy own sake, O my God*
Daniel 9:19

Christlike Compassion

Merely sharing another's burden is noble. To share it cheerfully is sublime.

Without distinction, without calculation, without procrastination, Love. Lavish it upon the poor, where it is very easy; especially upon the rich, who often need it most; most of all, upon our equals, where it is very difficult, and for whom perhaps we each do least of all.

—Henry Drummond

THE WORLD GOES ON WITHOUT US

Just yesterday I shopped
For groceries here as usual;
Today the door is locked
But it's a kind refusal.
Beneath the wreath it says,
"Last night of heart attack
The owner passed away";
Lord! what a tragic fact!
Such wreaths always surprise,
But it's a kind refusal
For underneath it reads,
"Business tomorrow as usual."

COMPENSATION

She loved the orphans' home
And often visited there,
And then one day she gave
To them her diamonds rare.
Friends say her gems are gone
But she always replies,
"I see them every day
Sparkling in children's eyes."

THOUGHTS FROM THE SLUMS

Shivering boys passed a church
And one waif asked, "What's that?"
The other said, "A church
Where Christians worship at."
"Then let's go in," he cried;
"It looks so warm in there."
"No! no!" the other said,
"They're having songs and prayer."
"Besides," the urchin said,
"Church-folk don't seem to be
Too much concerned about
Poor kids like you and me."

GIVE AND YOU SHALL RECEIVE

With vision dim I led
A man all blind to light,
And my dim eyes returned
To nearly perfect sight.
With shoulders stooped and tired
I shared my neighbor's load,
And strength came back to me
As I trudged up his road.
With failing faith I prayed
For one whose faith was gone,
And faith returned to me
As silent as the dawn.

Anyone who does not have the Spirit of Christ does not belong to him. **Romans 8:9**

Churches That Challenge

The church is not a gallery for the exhibition of eminent Christians, but a school for the education of imperfect ones. **Henry Ward Beecher**

CHURCHES OFFER CHRIST

She said, "A happy life
Is that for which I search,
But Preacher, I'm not sure
It's only found at church.
My clubs inspire me so
And oft while sitting there
I ask what churches preach
That lodges do not share."
He smiled, "Clubs meet a need
And add great zest to life,
But they don't even claim
To offer Jesus Christ."

A DERELICT SHIP

How can America
Seek providential care
While we ignore God's laws
And turn from faith and prayer?
Can we reject His love
And turn from His command
And still feel God is bound
To bless and save this land?
Can we Americans
Reject God's law so strict,
Without the ship of state
Becoming derelict?

If absence makes the heart grow fonder, think
how much some people must love the church.

WHAT MAKES A CHURCH?

You cannot build Christ's Church on earth
Around some preacher's fame,
Nor lifting up a lofty spire
Or painting on a name.
You cannot build Christ's Church on earth
With bricks, though laid with care
Nor with fine pews and carpets thick,
Nor with an organ rare.
His Church is built where He imparts
A portion of His Spirit,
So when the Word of God is read
Each humble heart can hear it.
His Church is built when true hearts blend
In prayer and hymns of praise,
So when God's Word is preached men see
Their Lord with loving gaze.
It is not built of spires and stones
Nor fancy choirs in tune;
Christ builds His great cathedral Church
Where two or three commune.

A BRIDGE TO BUILD

If earth spurns brotherhood
Another choice is given—
The massacre of mankind
Will damn us to oblivion.
And when the bombs come down
They will obliterate
With fiery holocaust
Our own United States.
What if within this age
We tried as hard to build
A bridge of brotherhood
As we do bombs that kill?

"On this rock I will build my church." **Matthew 16:18**

Consider the Children

To insure the education of teen-agers, let parents pull a few wires—like TV, telephone, radio and ignition.　　　　　　**Lavonne Mathison**

OUR CHILDREN'S WORLD

Why do we each forget
About our children's world,
Where harsh injustice stings
Each tiny boy and girl?
Why do we each forget
The world we left too soon,
Forgetting tears we shed
For every childhood wound.
Lest by injustice we
Should crush one boy or girl,
God, let us ne'er forget
About our children's world.

Every boy, in his heart, would rather steal second base than an automobile.

CHILDREN REMEMBER

The pleasures that you give
To boys and girls today
Will bring them happiness
When years have passed away.
For kindly words you speak
And loving deeds you do
Will warm their hearts for years
And they'll remember you.
But break one childish heart,
And when that child is grown
He'll not forget your name
Though fifty years have flown.

THE END PRODUCT

I know as a parent
I have my choice
Of being more agreeable
And softening my voice,
'Til I, undemanding
Am praised unending
By children untaught
Who lack understanding.
But forfeiting popularity
To enforce discipline,
I know in the end
I'll raise good citizens.

LET THE CHILDREN IN

Church doors are heavy doors
As all churchgoers learn
And church door knobs are all
Too high for kids to turn.
Last week outside our church
I watched my child, aged four,
Trying in vain to reach
The knob on our church door.
I thought as I reached down
To help my small beginner,
"Why aren't church doors planned so
Small boys and girls can enter?"

But Jesus called them to him, saying, "Let the children come to me, and do not hinder them; for to such belongs the kingdom of God."
Luke 18:16

Convictions That Count

The courage we desire and prize is not the courage
to die decently but to live manfully.

Thomas Carlyle

A man should share the action and passion of his times at the peril of being judged not to have lived.　　　　—Oliver Wendell Holmes

ONE FEAR

I met an ancient man
With weary steps and slow;
I asked him where he'd been
And where he planned to go.
"I've been in life's great war,"
I heard the man reply,
"And dauntless I go forth
To battle till I die."
"Have you no fear?" I asked.
He said, "I'm fear-possessed
That I will flee my post
When Duty asks my best."

VAIN PILGRIMAGE

Some visit Jacob's well
And drink from Sychar's fount,
And some stand where Christ preached
His Sermon on the Mount.
To stand where Jesus preached
Inspiring with His thought,
Is vain unless back home
You live by truth He taught.

HONESTY IS DYING HERE

I know what this world needs.
It needs true-blue, honest people;
I mean a hundred percent,
And as straight as a steeple.
We've pussyfooted too long,
Smiling on falsehood,
Dealing in half-truths,
Compromising good.
Our land will be free as long
As Americans are true
But when honesty dies out here,
So freedom dies, too.

MEN WANTED

Of squeamish-minded men
I want to have no part,
And men with priggish views
So niggardly at heart.
For pygmy-minded men
Embracing midget goals
Squelch cherished faith from me
Just as they blight all souls.
Of stingy-minded men
My weary heart is tiring;
God, give us braver men,
Great-hearted and inspiring.

To realize God's presence is the one sovereign remedy against temptation.

My heart is steadfast, O God, my heart is steadfast!
Psalms 108:1

Courage That Cheers

Had Moses waited until he understood how Israel could elude Pharaoh's armies, they might have been in Egypt still. **Martin Luther**

When you conclude a thing may not be achieved, look up and you'll probably see someone doing it.

WHEN COUNTING FOR SOMETHING

A boy longing to count for something
Passed by a leaking dike
And sensed his lifetime chance had come
To count and be useful-like.
He saw and quickly took his chance
To save the Netherlands
By plugging a very tiny leak
Using one finger on a hand.
Through the frozen night he stood fast
Crying aloud for help
And willing, if it were necessary,
To sacrifice himself.
Dutchmen claim he saved their country
And when nursed back to life
He said, "When counting for something,
Boys don't mind sacrifice."

No Christian can be a pessimist, for Christianity is a system of radical optimism.
—William R. Inge

BALANCING THE BOOK

When saddened by slow progress
I think of where I'm from,
Of obstacles surmounted,
And just how far I've come.
When failure dogs my steps
With tasks left half-way finished,
I recount victories won
And pleasures undiminished.
When from my poor performance
Remorse is unrelieved,
I balance my book of failures
With triumphs I've achieved.

THE MINISTRY OF PAIN

Dear Christ, who tasted death
Refusing to complain,
But used Your cross to bless;
May I not do the same?
But how can my rude cross
Become a means of gain?
And how can I fulfill
A ministry of pain?
Lord, help me bravely bear
The cross You've given me,
And suffer with the faith
You proved at Calvary.

Because he cleaves to me in love, I will deliver him; I will protect him, because he knows my name. When he calls to me, I will answer him; I will be with him in trouble, I will rescue him and honor him. **Psalms 91:14, 15**

Dad's Dilemma

It's funny how parents obey their children these days.

IN DAD'S FOOTSTEPS

There goes my Dad and am I proud
That I am one of his,
And when I'm grown I plan to be
A man just like he is.
He never has to go to church
On any Sabbath day,
And when we bow for mealtime grace
He never has to pray.
He says some words I can't use yet
But I remember them,
And when I'm grown I'll say them too,
And learn to curse like him.
Of course, by then, like Dad I'll be
Too big to go to church,
Though even now I dread to go
And hate it very much.
Not even Mother knows my plan
For she would not be glad
To know I hope to be someday
A man just like my Dad.
Yes, there's my Dad and I am proud
That I am one of his;
Today I walk in his footsteps,
Soon I'll be what he is.

⚜

If you must hold yourself up to your children as an object lesson, hold yourself up as a warning and not as an example.

The great, the astonishing thing about youth is that it may be enjoyed twice! Once through one's own youth and later and better through that of another.
　　　　　　　　　—Phillip Barry

The best safeguard of the younger generation is a good example by the older generation.

WAITING AT THE GATE

When I came home from work
I'd see him by the gate,
For just at sunset time
My little boy would wait.
I always scooped him up,
His cheek against my cheek,
And oft I pressed a kiss
On one too thrilled to speak.
But my small boy grew tall
And marks of manhood bore,
And boyhood years took flight
To come back nevermore.
Now by that gate I see
No more my little man,
And yet I'm sure it's all
A part of God's great plan.
Yet I'd give all I have
To meet my boy again,
Waiting at the gate
When weary workdays end.

Fathers, do not provoke your children to anger, but bring them up in the discipline and instruction of the Lord.
　　　　　　　　　Ephesians 6:4

Daily Devotions

He stands best who kneels most.

A MAN SHOULD PAUSE

A man should pause each passing day
And try his best to see
If he's the man his mother thought
He'd someday grow to be.
A man should stop most every day
And hug the kids who're his
And ask himself if he's as true
As they believe he is.
A man should halt his pace each day
And probe his inner life
To see if he lives by ideals
Expected of his wife.
A man should search his heart each day
From dawn 'til twilight dim
To see if what he has become
Is what God planned for him.

Prayer is the most important thing in my life. If
I should neglect prayer for a single day, I should
lose a great deal of the fire of faith.
——Martin Luther

THE PERFECT DAY

I felt the touch of God at dawn
And faith revived when guilt was gone.
I felt the breath of God at noon.
And worries ,fled as love came soon.
I felt the hush of God this eve
And God's sweet peace bade tiredness leave.
Today I've dared to walk with God
And romance crowned the path I trod.

When I pray coincidences happen and when I do
not, they don't.   ——William Temple

I SMILED AT GOD

Her source of beauty rare
He sought to know one day,
And so he trailed her to
The church where she would pray.
She left with face aglow
And he spoke with a nod,
"What is your beauty's source?"
And she replied, "It's God."
He said, "Will you explain?"
She cried, "On bended knee,
Each day I smile at God,
And He smiles back at me."

A PLACE FOR MENDING THINGS

It's not a waste of time
When reapers pause to file,
In laden harvest fields,
A sickle blade or scythe.
Nor is a fisherman
Entitled to regret
The time he uses up
When mending his torn net.
Nor is prayer-time a waste
If it a blessing brings;
It's just a sharpening time,
A place for mending things.

Every day I will bless thee, and praise thy name
for ever and ever.   **Psalms 145:2**

Dedicated Disciples

*The followers of Jesus learn not a theory so much
as experience a Presence; embrace not a doctrine
so much as enter a fellowship.*

Some Christians are like porcupines. They have
many fine points but it's hard to get next to them.
—Vance Havner

WHAT IS A CHRISTIAN?

Frail arms by which Christ lifts,
Weak lips by which He speaks,
A heart through which He loves
And feet by which He seeks.
A soul indwelt by Christ
And eyes through which He sees,
A mind that thinks His thoughts
And hands that strive to please.
A life where Jesus lives,
A will which He commands;
A yielded mind and heart,
Surrendered feet and hands.

Some churchmembers are good in two ways—no
good and good for nothing.

The Christian is not one who has gone all the
way with Christ, none of us has. The Christian
is one who has found the right road.
—Charles L. Allen

GREAT PLANS

One said, "It yet remains
To see what God can do
With one who fully yields
To Christ, the Savior true."
I said, "I'll yield my life
And all I am to Thee—
And all I've ever been
And all I hope to be."
Christ said, "Then I'll bless you
Although your gifts are few;
And you'd be proud to know
Of plans I have for you."

I'M GLAD I FOLLOWED

I heard Him calling me
And I obeyed and came
To champion His cause
And stand up for His name.
I soon found paths were rough
And yet through troubled days
I followed nail-scarred steps
And I learned to love His ways.
I'm glad I followed Him
Though costly was the price,
And could I take it back
I'd choose again for Christ.

*For he was a good man, full of the Holy Spirit
and of faith.* **Acts 11:24**

Deeds of Duty

Duty is the sublimest word in our language.

Robert E. Lee

The two most beautiful things in the universe are the starry heavens above our hands, and the feeling of duty in our hearts.

IT CAN'T BE DONE

I most admire him who can cry
"It can't be done but I will try."
Who shouts as he his goals pursues,
"What can't be done is what I'll do!"
Who sings this song once he's begun,
"I do the things which can't be done!"
And then exclaims with joy unhid,
"What can't be done is what I did."

To do one's duty sounds a rather cold and cheerless business, but somehow in the end it does give one a queer sort of satisfaction.

—Somerset Maugham

SAY IT NOW

If I were sure I had
One final day on earth,
I'd spend it telling friends
How much to me they're worth.
If I were sure I had
Just one more hour grim,
I'd spend it telling friends
How much I cherish them.
I'd speak to friends of love
If I had just one minute,
But since we never know,
I'll even now begin it.

THE AUCTION BLOCK

When men were bought and sold
A man addressed a slave,
"If I buy you, will you
Be faithful, true and brave?"
He said, "Though I'm a slave
And serfdom is my lot,
I will be true and brave
If you buy me or not."

So you also, when you have done all that is commanded you, say, "We are unworthy servants; we have only done what was our duty."

Luke 17:10

Difficult Decisions

It is easy to dodge our responsibilities but we cannot dodge the consequences of dodging our responsibilities. **Josiah Stamp**

IN RETROSPECT

The irony of my life
Is that my earthly days
Have all been spent going
Unknown, unchosen ways,
And doing work which I
Had never planned to do,
And living in some towns
Of which I never knew.
Yet, strangely, life thus lived
Need not be life misspent,
For mine in retrospect
Seems like the life God meant.

Next to knowing when to seize an opportunity, the most important thing in life is to know when to forego an advantage.

NEUTRALITY

He who can silent stand
When truth is being tried,
Withholding facts he knows,
Afraid to take a side,
Will find he's being judged
By truth confronting him,
And for his coward act
He'll find himself condemned;
Condemned to hell on earth
Deserved and unbegrudged,
Because he silent stood
When truth was being judged.

When you have to make a choice and don't make it, that is in itself a choice. —William James

THAT, INDEED, IS LIFE

If you can venture all
Upon some cherished plan
And then lose everything,
But take it like a man;
If you can wager all
Upon some daring scheme,
Only to lose your bet,
But not the gift to dream;
Then you can say you've lived,
Though cowards call it strife—
You've had the best there is,
For that, indeed, is life.

You can pretty accurately judge a man by whether he would ask for a light burden or a strong back if he were given the choice.

There are times when silence is golden, and there are times when silence is yellow. It is high time the church found out which is which.

Multitudes, multitudes, in the valley of decision!
For the day of the Lord is near in the valley of decision. **Joel 3:14**

Discipline and Determination

There has never yet been a man in our history who led a life of ease whose name is worth remembering. **Theodore Roosevelt**

One of the reasons why you need no special education to be a Christian is that Christianity is an education in itself. —C. S. Lewis

God provides food for every bird but he doesn't toss it into the mouth.

I'LL BE LIVING PROOF

Dear God, who made all things
And made most things appear
To grow in elegance
With every passing year,
Please beautify my life
And crown it with Thy grace
So that old age finds me
Reflecting Jesus' face,
And glorifying Thee
So that when I grow old
None thinks of seeing me
But sees Christ in my soul.
If You should grant me this
And by Thy Presence strengthen
Then I will fear no more
When evening shadows lengthen.
But I'll be living proof
That if one does his duty
You'll keep your promise, God,
To touch old age with beauty.

THE REACH OF PRAYER

What lies beyond the reach of prayer?
Does help for those who're ill?
Oh no! But only that which lies
Outside the Father's will.
What lies beyond the reach of prayer?
Does grace for life's demands?
Oh, no! But only that which lies
Outside the Father's plans.
What lies beyond the reach of prayer?
Does strength from Heaven above?
Oh no! But only that which lies
Outside the Father's love.
What lies beyond the reach of prayer?
Does faith each day to start?
Oh no! But only that which lies
Outside God's gracious heart.

Everything comes to him who hustles while he waits. —Thomas A. Edison

Spade deeper and dig deeper if you want your life to be a bed of roses.

It is not the number of hours that a man puts in, but what a man puts in the hours that counts.

We are afflicted in every way, but not crushed; perplexed, but not driven to despair.
2 Corinthians 4:8

appy is he whose help is the God of Jacob, whose hope is in the Lord his God, who made heaven and earth, the sea, and all that is in them; who keeps faith for ever. . . .

Psalms 146:5–6

CHRIST'S OTHER WORD

If I had said, "Go fight for faith,"
You would have volunteered,
And if I'd said, "Debate your faith,"
You would have loudly cheered.
If I had said, "Defend your faith,"
You would, no doubt, have done it,
Or even if I'd said, "Go preach,"
You'd doubtless have begun it.
But since I said, "Go live your faith
And live so none can doubt,"
You said, though not in speech or script,
"Lord, you can count me out."

And whatever you ask in prayer, you will receive, if you have faith.   **Matthew 21:22**

Educational Experience

*Some people use Christianity like a bus; they ride
on it only when it is going their way.*

PRAYING HANDS

The Master understands my words
When I attempt to pray,
But hands uplifted oft express
Some thoughts too deep to say.
That's why, dear Lord, I lift these hands
Though they're not scarred like Thine;
Yet Master when my prayer's unclear
Behold these hands of mine.

"Oh, Lord, give me a back-bone as big as a saw log, and ribs like the sleepers under the church floor; put iron shoes on me, and galvanized breeches. And give me a rhinoceros hide for a skin, and hang a wagon load of determination up in the gable-end of my soul, and help me to sign the contract to fight the devil as long as I've got a fist, and bite him as long as I've got a tooth, and then gum him till I die. All this I ask for Christ's sake! AMEN"

—Bud Robinson

ATTITUDE COUNTS

Completely unaware
That I was judging him,
I watched a cripple pass
On dwarfed and twisted limb.
With pity in my heart
I seemed to hear One say,
"As you are judging him
You're being judged today."
"What do you mean?" I asked.
He cried, "Each one, indeed
Is judged by attitudes
Expressed toward souls in need."

Again and again I have been tempted to give up the struggle, but always the figure of the strange man hanging upon the cross sends me back to my task again.   —Meister Eckhart

POSTSCRIPT OF LOVE

Each dawn and noon God speaks,
And had we ears to hear it
He would reveal His love
In language of the Spirit.
And then at sunset time
At the closing of the day,
God signs His signature
In love's own golden way.
But what of darkest nights
Bejeweled with stars above?
I have deciphered them
As God's postscript of love.

I put no value on anything I possess save in terms of the Kingdom of God.

*For the commandment is a lamp and the teaching
a light, and the reproofs of discipline are the way
of life.*   **Proverbs 6:23**

Effective Examples

If you wish your neighbors to see what God is like,
let them see what He can make you like.

Charles Kingsley

Many Christians have a burning desire to help suffering humanity except for those unfortunates they happen to know personally.

THE GAME OF LIFE

You may at half-time rest
And freshen up a bit,
But in the game of life
You can't afford to quit.
You may be sidelined now
To catch a breath or two,
But you can't stay there long;
The game is not half through.
You may call for time out
But don't you dare forget,
The game must be resumed
And you can't quit quite yet.

Bread cast upon the water after many days returns, usually with jam on it.

FOR CHRIST

In garments white a nurse so fair
Nursed lepers with such love and care
That she oft kissed their hands impaired
And smiled at them as if she cared.
"Millions in gold," exclaimed someone
"Would not make me do what you've done."
She said, "I too would spurn that price
But gladly I do this for Christ."

WHAT SAINTS ARE

The stained glass windows in our church
Cast saints in colors bright,
And sun shines through those images
Flooding our church with light.
So living saints are like the ones
Produced in stained-glass art;
Through them the light of God shines bright
And falls on every heart.

I MET A MAN

When I was looking down
And bitter was my cup,
I met a man of faith
Who left me looking up.
When I was down and out
And everything went wrong,
I met a man of joy
Who left me with a song.
When I was "all done in"
And fear had drained strength out,
I met a man of faith
Who cancelled every doubt.
And I left him that day
With head uplifted high,
Thanking God for men
Who challenge and inspire.

We're often remorseful for speaking harshly but have you ever heard of one regretful for speaking kindly?

Set the believers an example in speech and conduct, in love, in faith, in purity.

1 Timothy 4:12

Enchanted Environment

Every now and then a man's mind is stretched by a new idea and never shrinks back to its original proportions. **Oliver Wendell Holmes**

TO SIMPLICITY AND BEAUTY

Let me return to simpler things
For I am now persuaded
I was not made for cluttered living
With paths too complicated.
Let me return to simpler things
Convinced amidst the strife,
I can't survive unless I find
The plainer path of life.
Lord, lead me from these tangled paths
Of complex days and duty,
And guide me down quiet paths of service
To simplicity and beauty.

WE OUGHT TO GET THEM BACK

Our old smokehouse that used to be
Exists no more for eye to see.
Smokehouses went like one-room schools
And turning-plows hitched up to mules.
We ought to get smokehouses back,
Smoke seeping out of every crack;
But they went out like fires we fixed
Of hickory chips and sassafras sticks.
Yet still I see in my mind's eye
Smokehouses filled with hams hung high
And smell again that fragrance good—
Smoke rising from ham-smoking wood.

Education is never as expensive as ignorance.

If a man empties his purse into his head, no man can take it away from him; an investment in knowledge pays the best interest.

—Benjamin Franklin

THE OLD HOMEPLACE

I've got to turn aside
From life's exhausting pace
And make a pilgrimage
Back to the old homeplace.
Familiar childhood paths
Through shady woods I'll roam,
And I at last shall stand
Upon the hills of home.
And there forgotten dreams,
Ideals that slipped away
Will all come marching back
When I go home today.
And I, refreshed, shall then
Turn back to life's mad race,
If only I today
Can see the old homeplace.

LAMPLIT ROOMS

We use to wash the chimney clean
And fill the lamp with kerosene.
We'd trim the wick and strike a match
And hold it 'til the light would catch.
And as the shades of night would fall
Lamplight so soft dispelled them all.
Nostalgic thoughts when darkness looms
Makes me homesick for lamplit rooms.

The earth is the Lord's and the fulness thereof, the world and those who dwell therein.

Psalms 24:1

Evangelistic Emphasis

The best commentary upon the Bible is a good life.

Is your Christianity ancient history or current events? —Samuel Shoemaker

Evangelism is to present Jesus Christ in the power of the Holy Spirit that men might come to trust Him as Saviour and serve Him as Lord in the fellowship of His Church.

—William Temple

MY OWN TRANSLATION

The scholars boldly say
They must translate again
The Book our Fathers loved
Which speaks of God to men.
And I am glad they plan
To do for us once more
What every age has done
A thousand times before.
And while I hold such men
In highest estimation,
Yet I, in my own way,
Must make my own translation.
Though not as scholars do—
Each day I now am giving
My version of God's word
Translated into living.

People take your example far more seriously than they do your advice.

AN OUNCE OF PRESSURE

I asked how he had found
The Saviour's great salvation,
And he quite thoughtfully
Returned this explanation:
"Beneath my coat lapel
Mild pressure was applied,
An ounce or two or less;
That won me for God's side."
"What do you mean?" I asked.
He said, "A Christian true
Gently pulled me toward him
And whispered, 'God needs you.'"

WHAT IS EVANGELISM?

I asked, "What is evangelism?"
A poor man kindly said,
"It's like a tramp who tells
A friend where he found bread."
I asked, "What is evangelism?"
A blind youth softly sighed,
"It's like a sightless man
Who loves to praise his guide."
I asked, "What is evangelism?"
An ill man quickly told,
"It's like one snatched from death
Telling who made him whole."

As for you, always be steady, endure suffering, do the work of an evangelist, fulfil your ministry.
2 Timothy 4:5

Everyday Enthusiasm

Years wrinkle your skin but to give up enthusiasm
wrinkles your soul. **Samuel Ullman**

If I were to begin life again I should want it as it was. I would only open my eyes a little more. —Jules Renard

Happiness comes when we sense we are of some use to somebody.

LEAVE A WINDOW

I love my daily task
Of washing dishes bright
For just above my sink
I have a window light.
And as I wash the plates
I glimpse the sky and sod
And when I lift my eyes
I lift my heart to God.
Were there no windows here
My work I could not bear,
But washing dishes now
Is just a time of prayer.
And may all builders strive
In building homes to think
To leave a window wide
Above the kitchen sink.

I do not know what your destiny will be, but one thing I know: the only ones among you who will be really happy are those who will have sought and found how to serve.
—Albert Schweitzer

What makes us discontented without condition is the absurdly exaggerated idea we have of the happiness of others.

Happiness is that peculiar sensation one gets when he is too busy to be miserable.

THESE THREE THINGS

Grant me some task to do
And strength enough to do it,
And grant me daring faith
To know that I'll stick to it.
Give me a heart to love
With love to splurge upon it,
And strength to give it up
If you, my Lord, should want it.
Grant me one hope and dream,
And courage to pursue it,
And lest I miss my goal
Dear God, please guide me to it.

THERE'LL BE ANOTHER DAY

When I have done my best and failed
There's one more thing to say,
"Though failures of the past remain,
There'll be another day."
And I'm pleased God planned life thus,
For when I've lost a fight,
I know there'll be another day
With ledger clean and white.
And what a hopeless world we'd face
If we could never say,
"Although I've made a mess of things,
There'll be another day."

But as for me and my house, we will serve the Lord. **Joshua 24:15**

Facing the Future

The farther backward you can look, the farther forward you are likely to see.

Winston Churchill

God is in the facts of history as truly as he is in the march of the seasons.

IT'S DAYS TO COME THAT MATTER

Live for the future, not the past!
The past is full of dread,
Or else of failure, guilt and fears;
Then let us look ahead!
Live for the future, not the past!
The past makes sad men sadder;
Past days and deed rehashed depress;
It's days to come that matter.
Live for the future, not the past
And you'll unlock life's mystery;
Exploits undreamed await our doing.
We yet may rewrite history.

BETTER FARTHER ON

Ready to quit, I cried,
"Oh, Lord, I'm all alone"
But from the gloom He spoke,
"It's better farther on."
Bowed low in shame I wept,
"Then give me one more day!"
And instantly gloom fled
And hope dawned on my way.
And walking in that light
Nor dreading the unknown,
I've found His words were true,
"It's better farther on."

A WORTHWHILE THING

If you'll think back you'll see
How blessings came to you,
Through woes which you endured
And troubles you passed through.
And present fears you face
You'll clearly see someday,
Were working for your good
To keep you in God's way.
And all your future years
With joys and woes they bring
Are but God's plan to make
Your life a worthwhile thing.

Today is the tomorrow we worried about yesterday.

DO BETTER NOW MY CHILD

Why should I weep at night
For things that might have been?
Tomorrow is the land
Of beginning again.
Why should I brood upon
Past days and deeds defiled?
Tomorrow God will say,
"Do better now, My child!"
Why should I fret and fuss
As if this were the end?
Tomorrow dawns the world
Of beginning again.

But one thing I do, forgetting what lies behind and straining forward to what lies ahead, I press toward the goal for the prize of the upward call of God in Christ Jesus. **Philippians 3:13, 14**

Faith Conquers Fear

Almost without exception, he who has put faith out of his heart has first put obedience out of his life.

The beginning of anxiety is the end of faith; and the beginning of true faith is the end of anxiety.

—George Mueller

There are a thousand ways of pleasing God, but not one without faith.

IT MATTERS WHAT YOU BELIEVE

Conclude you're beat and it will be!
Believe you can withstand,
And you will get a spurt of strength
To win a victory grand.
Conclude you're through and you'll soon quit,
But say you can't retire,
And you'll find strength to win new heights
That most folk can't acquire.
Conclude you're done and hope takes flight!
Believe you'll find the way,
And you'll soon find the darkest night
Dawning into day.
Conclude you're old and you'll give up,
But think young like a youth
And faith will let you do exploits
And blaze new trails of truth.
For one's belief affects his life,
And all our faith and fears
And doubts and false beliefs, as well
Fashion our latter years.

Feed your faith and your doubts will starve to death.

Being religious means asking passionately the questions of our existence and being willing to receive answers even if the answers hurt.

—Paul Tillich

THE LITTLE CARES

I pray about big things
That threaten me each day,
And then for little cares
I often fail to pray.
I pray about grave ills
That steal my peace of mind
But seldom do I pray
About the lesser kind.
But since God knows my need
And sees my every care,
I wonder why I hide
Small things from God in prayer.

WHAT IS WORRY FOR?

If worry were worthwhile
Or paid a single debt,
I'm sure it would be right
To worry, fume, and fret.
If it could make it rain
Or make a person rich,
Then I would lie awake
Each night to toss and pitch.
Then what is worry for
If worry doesn't pay?
I think it's just a sign
We've failed to trust and pray.

Fear not, for I am with you, be not dismayed, for I am your God; I will strengthen you, I will help you, I will uphold you with my victorious right hand.

Isaiah 41:10

Faultfinding Is Foolish

Most people enjoy the inferiorities of their best friends.

GENEROUS TO OTHERS' FAULTS

The best of all your traits
Which I see greatness in,
Is your forgiving spirit
You show to erring men.
Not once have your chaste lips
Repeated scandals heard,
For you still put the best
Construction on harsh words.
If only everyone
Could have at least one friend
Who's always generous to
The faults of sinning men.

WHY SCOLD?

The man was unaware
The shine-boy had bad news
When he went in and asked
The lad to shine his shoes.
And as he tried to shine
And never ceased from trying,
The man began to scold
'Til he heard that lad crying.
When he saw his shoes soaked
With tears from his small brother,
He felt remorse when told,
"Last week, I lost my mother."

Faultfinders never improve things; they just make things seem worse than they really are.

What people say behind your back is your standing in the community.   —Edgar Watson Howe

When I was young I resolved not to get married until I met the ideal woman. Some years later I found her but she was looking for the ideal man.
—Michel Simon

SPITE FENCE

With anger in my heart
I built one night a wall
Between my house and his,
And it was very tall.
I planned to see no more
The man I'd learned to hate,
And so I left no gap
To hang a friendly gate.
And though we met no more,
That fence to my surprise
Cast shadows on my lawn
And hid from me sunrise.

Correcting faults is like tying a necktie; we can do it easier on ourselves than on anybody else.

To the pure all things are pure, but to the corrupt and unbelieving nothing is pure.   **1 Titus 1:15**

Forgetting Failure

How a person plays the game shows something of his character. How he loses shows all of it.

Failure is only the opportunity to begin again, more intelligently.   —Henry Ford

TO FAILURES

Though some exalt the one
Who wins the victor's prize,
I praise the one who fails,
Although he tries and tries.
Hats off to those who've failed,
Yet dare to try again;
It takes more strength to lose
Than is required to win.
And I salute with pride
Brave souls who're not denying
That life has passed them by,
But they go right on trying.

QUICKLY RISE

If in the mire you fall
While marching into town,
For goodness sake don't quit
Because you've fallen down.
So if in living life
You should fall into sin
You must get quickly up
And start the trip again.
But you, if you fall down
Will be by life outsmarted
Unless you quickly rise
And by God's help get started.

ANOTHER CHANCE

Give me tomorrow, Lord,
And I'll use it for Thee,
And make You proud You gave
Tomorrow unto me.
Give me tomorrow, Lord,
For I have failed today
To do what I should do
And say what I should say.
Give me tomorrow, Lord,
And I'll return to You
A day crammed full of deeds
Which I have failed to do.

God is more anxious to forgive the blotted page of endeavor than the blank page of surrender.

ONE STEP MORE

When you are all "done in,"
Faced with a failing score,
There's one thing more to do,
Try taking one step more.
When you've thrown up your hands
Without a friend to help,
There's one thing more to do,
Try taking one more step.
When you've been counted out
There's one thing more to do;
Get up and start again,
Take one more step or two.

Why do you cry to me? Tell the people of Israel to go forward.   **Exodus 14:15**

Friends and Fellowship

We make more enemies by what we say than friends by what we do.   **John Collins**

Our worst enemies are often the friends we once talked to as only a friend should.

Nobody can have too many friends but one enemy constitutes a surplus.

ACCEPTANCE IS ITS THEME

Friendship is much much more
Than words for friendship's sake;
It's more than smiles and grins
Mixed with a warm handshake.
And friendship's more than gifts
Exchanged on festive days,
And it goes far beyond
Mere words and deeds of praise.
Friendship is being kind
To 'one with shattered dreams,
And loving him in spite
Of all his failing schemes.
It's bearing someone's shame
When others would not dare,
And sharing someone's grief
When others fail to care.
Of course such friendship costs—
It was not cheap for Christ.
Acceptance is its theme;
Involvement is the price.

Like spokes in a wheel, we're closer to each other as we draw closer to Christ, the center of life.

I CALL YOU FRIEND

I call you friend
For that portrays my feeling,
And it, upon reflection,
Is a word appealing.
Friend, you've shared my joys
And in my troubles, helped.
You've laughed when I've rejoiced
And suffered when I wept.
I call you friend
For it depicts so true
What I would like to be
If I could be like you.

THE KEY TO FRIENDSHIP

To enter friendship's door
I sought a key to fit;
I tried the key of wealth
But could not enter it.
I tried the key of fame,
And pleasure's golden key,
But friendship's door so wide
Would not unlock for me.
But when I tried one key
And gave the door a shove
I watched it open wide,
Because the key was love.

A friend loves at all times.   **Proverbs 17:17**

Genuine Greatness

*Big men become big by doing what they didn't
want to do when they didn't want to do it.*

THAT WE MIGHT WALK IN BEAUTY

Oh, Thou unhurried Christ, who trod
The irksome path of duty,
Help us to walk unhurried ways
That we might walk in beauty.
For in Thy calm resolve, dear Christ,
And in Thy mind unworried,
We note how much Your life achieved
Unfretful and unhurried.
So let us follow Thee who was
Involved in such self-giving
That we, unrushed, shall imitate
The calmness of Thy living.

IT GLEAMED THROUGH THORNS

A person's greatness can't be hid
But comes in many forms;
Sometimes it comes through sunshine days,
Sometimes it comes through storms.
A person's greatness is revealed
In many, many ways;
Sometimes it shines when we are cursed,
Sometimes it's when we're praised.
A person's greatness will be seen
When fame his name adorns;
Sometimes it comes in other ways;
For Christ it gleamed through thorns.

Sometime in your life you will meet a truly great
man who could not care less for money or fame.
Then you will know how poor you really are.

TRUE GREATNESS

With Lincoln I would be
A great emancipator,
Or speak like Henry Clay
The gallant legislator.
I would like Washington
Insure this land's survival,
Or even like Saint Paul
Promote a world revival.
But such is not God's will!
Yet in my world I'll be
Well-pleasing, doing work
The Master's given me.

There is in every man something greater than he
had begun to dream of. Men are nobler than they
think themselves.   —Phillips Brooks

Great minds have noble objectives, high pur-
poses, and daring dreams; average minds engage
themselves with wishful thinking and petty dab-
blings in little ventures; small minds are content
to complain why life passed them by.

*Behold, the Lord our God has shown us his glory
and greatness.*   **Deuteronomy 5:24**

hey still bring forth fruit in old age. . . .   **Psalms 92:14**

OLD AGE REVEALS

Is isn't easy growing old,
But now I know it's true,
Old age reveals what youth conceals
Of strength to see you through.
God's bright designs blend beautifully
As they through life have done,
And through dark days God guides us when
Dark clouds conceal the sun.
It isn't easy growing old,
But faith and hope up-springing
Have made these years, of all years, best—
And days of joyful singing.

Let no one despise your youth, but set the be-
lievers an example in speech and conduct, in love,
in faith, in purity.   **1 Timothy 4:12**

Gift of Gratitude

Gratitude is a duty which ought to be paid, but which none has a right to expect. **Rousseau**

When we were children we were grateful to those who filled our stockings with joy at Christmas time. Why are we not grateful to God for filling our stockings with legs.

—G. K. Chesterton

WE SELDOM OFFER PRAISE

An ancient legend states
That God sends forth each day
Two angels who collect
Each word of prayer we pray.
One bears a basket large
On snowy angel wings,
And it o'er flows each day
With prayers requesting things.
The other angel comes
To earth with basket small
And gathers up the prayers
Of thanks from one and all.
And as the legend goes
On sturdy wings and skilled,
He leaves the earth each day
With basket seldom filled.
If such a legend's true—
As it indeed may be—
I wonder what God thinks
Of folk like you and me.
We all have offered up
Some prayer request for days,
But when the answer comes
We seldom offer praise.

MY DEBT TO NEIGHBORS

Within my neighbor's yard
There grows a giant oak tree
And with wide limbs it casts
Shade on my house and me.
Without permit my bees
Go gather nectar up
From neighbor's flower beds
Of "mums" and buttercups.
Within my tree-cooled yard
I oft rest from my labors,
Or eating honey comb
I sense my debt to neighbors.

All our discomforts spring from the want of thankfulness for what we have.

ON CREDIT

Life is a credit deal,
And we receive each day
Blessings extravagant,
Too great for us to pay.
But debts incurred leave not
A one of us exempt
From paying what we can;
At least we should attempt.
But what can one man do?
I know how I'll repay;
On debts so large I'll make
Small payments every day.

Love one another with brotherly affection; outdo one another in showing honor. **Romans 12:10**

Goodness of God

The image under which the Nature of God can best be conceived is that of tender care that nothing be lost.   **Alfred North Whitehead**

It is a mistake to assume that God is interested only, or even chiefly, in religion.

—William Temple

IT'S GOOD BECAUSE IT'S HIS

God squanders not one thing
Of leaves or sun or frost,
For in His plan no twig
Or sprig of grass is lost.
And in His plan I know
No soul is made in vain,
Although for me at times
His purpose is not plain.
But I shall know someday
Just what His purpose is,
And in the meantime trust
It's good because it's His.

GREATER THAN YOU DREAM

Can God who flung each star
From flaming fingertips,
Watch one so frail as I
Lest one of my feet slips?
I know the God who arched
The skies and earthly ball
And paints each lily fair
And sees each sparrow fall.
Some say, "But God's too great
To care for earth's sad scheme."
I say, "Your God's too small.
He's greater than you dream!"

When our clever sciences are forgotten, when all other stories fall, when the earth waxes old like a garment, the Gospel will still be young; it will still have power to untangle our raveled life; it will still win us to our heart's true home.

—George Buttrick

BUT HE IS GOD

If God is God and God is good
And if He has all power,
And if He's wise and kind and just
Then I can face this hour.
If God is God and God is good
And if I am His child,
And if He's true and great and fair
Then I can face this trial.
If God is God and God is good
And present everywhere,
And if He sees each sparrow fall
Then I my cross can bear.
If God is God—but He is God
And He forgives all sin,
Then there is hope for souls like me.
God, let me try again!

The New Testament does not say "You shall know the rules and by them you shall be bound," but "You shall know the truth and the truth shall make you free."   —John Baillie

Ascribe to the Lord the glory due his name.
Psalms 96:8

Growing in Gladness

No joy is complete unless it is shared.

KEEPING A PLEASURE BOOK

She had her cup of grief,
For troubles came to her
But she ignored them all
Like they did not occur.
She would forget bad things,
But things that made her glad
Were all recorded in
A Pleasure Book she had.
She memorized that book,
And people bless her yet
For in her Pleasure Book
She knew what to forget.

I have found that most people are about as
happy as they make up their minds to be.

—A. Lincoln

JUST REHEARSING

May it be said of me
When I bow from life's stage,
"He played with all his heart
The role he should have played."
May it be said of me
When life's last curtains fall,
"He played his part with zest
Although his part was small."
And may I hear God say
When from the stage I bow,
"Rehearsal days are done;
Your starring role starts now."

Happiness is no easy matter; it is very hard to
find it within ourselves, and impossible to find it
anywhere else.

Remember the steam kettle, though up to its
neck in hot water, continues to sing.

YOUNG AT HEART

If you should say I'm old
Then I would say you're wrong;
And though my sight is dim
My heart is young and strong.
If you should think I'm old,
Don't breathe it with your tongue,
For though my back is bent
My heart is brave and young.
If you should think I'm old,
I may agree in part;
My body did grow old
But I stayed young at heart.

Happiness in this world, when it comes, comes
incidentally.—Make it the object of pursuit, and
it leads us a wild-goose chase, and is never at-
tained.

—Nathaniel Hawthorne

The Lord has done great things for us; we are glad.
Psalms 126:3

Guidance Through Grief

*Growing spiritually is like tea: it takes hot water
to bring out the best.*

Great trials seem to be a necessary preparation
for great duties. —E. Thomson

SOMEDAY I'LL KNOW FOR SURE

Someday I hope to read
The meaning of my tears
And with a clear insight
See through my shattered years.
Someday I'd like to know
Why disappointments came,
And why when some won "big"
I lost all but my shame.
Someday I'd like to scan
My life from first 'til last
And grasp God's reason for
The storms through which I've passed.
Still faith I claim tells me
That all things I endure
Are fragments of God's plan;
Someday I'll know for sure.

Blessed to us is the night, for it reveals the stars
to us.

If God sends us on strong paths, He will provide
us with strong shoes. —Alexander Maclaren

MORE THAN I PLANNED

Too long I ran my life,
Until the woes life brings
Made me conclude at last
I was just ruining things.
'Twas then Christ said, "I'll help;
It's much too soon to quit;
I can do more with life
Than you can do with it."
'Twas then my life distressed
Was placed at His command,
And He's achieved through me
Much more than I had planned.

God gets his best soldiers out of the highlands of
affliction.

I have lived a long life and I have known lots of
trouble but most of it never occurred.

BIRDS FIND THE SUNNY SOUTH

God grants a restlessness
To birds in winterlands,
To flee through pathless skies,
And guides them with His hand.
God grants a restlessness
To men who should respond,
And some on wings of faith
Fly toward their home beyond.
For men like helpless birds
Are called to flee from strife.
Birds find the sunny south,
Men find eternal life.

*For godly grief produces a repentance that leads
to salvation and brings no regret, but wordly grief
produces death.* **2 Corinthians 7:10**

Happy Homes

Children seldom step on the toes of parents who put their feet down firmly.

TO SHARE A WORLD OF LOVE

I've never been abroad
Or spanned the spacious seas,
Or scaled the mountains tall
Or felt the Arctic freeze.
But here in childhood paths
With home scenes loved so dear,
Fate has decreed it seems
That I should linger near.
What though I am denied
Luxury, wealth or ease?
I think of me as blest
And wealthy if you please.
I've known the love of children;
I've had a loyal wife;
I've loved my neighbors dearly;
I've tasted deep of life.
To share a world of love
Makes me not feel offended
That I've not been abroad;
My narrow world is splendid.

THE YARD I LOVE

Here in my own back yard
I own a little world
Composed of drowsy bees
And a perky little squirrel.
When blue jays taunt my wrens
Some sparrows come to chase,
And warty toads intrude
As if they owned the place.
Some terrapins hide out here;
One time I fed a dove,
And rabbits take shortcuts
Across the yard I love.

A small house can hold as much love as a bigger one.

THE NEAREST THING TO HEAVEN

Home is the place we turn
At closing of the day,
Where fellowship restores
The strength that's drained away.
Home is the spot we seek
With love that fonder grows
For friends wait there we love
And we are loved by those.
Home is a reverent place
That grows each year more reverend—
The dearest place on earth
The nearest thing to heaven.

CHILDREN CRAVE LOVE

When they realized that to their home
No children would be born
They visited in an orphan's home
And saw a boy forlorn.
The child appealed to them so much
She gave to him a toy
And softly asked, "Would you consent
To be my little boy?"
He gazed at her with searching gaze
Until she finally said,
"Oh, I'll give you a lot of toys,
A bike and wagon red."
When she named many things she'd buy
That average boys enjoy,
She was surprised when he inquired,
"But could you love a boy?"

For God commanded, "Honor your father and your mother." **Matthew 15:4**

Heroes Are Human

Most heroes emerge not from halls of luxury but
from dark paths of suffering and persecution.

Many men owe the grandeur of their lives to their tremendous difficulties.

—Charles Spurgeon

WHAT IS COURAGE?

I know what courage is:
It's fear that hums a tune;
It's doubt that offers prayers;
It's mirth in face of gloom.
It's tear-stained cheeks that smile
And calmness when you're cursed,
And courage is defeat
That quotes a Scripture verse.
It's singing in the dark,
"The dawn will be so bright";
It's saying when you're blind,
"I see without my sight."
It's seamen tossed at sea
With nothing left to do
But shout above the storm,
"We'll hold the rudder true."

God's giants have been weak men who did great things for God because they reckoned on His being with them.   —Hudson Taylor

HEROES ARE NOT EXEMPT FROM FEAR

A man should do his duty when
He's least inclined to do it,
And stand beside his post when it's
Not easy to stick to it.
A man should pray the hardest when
His soul can hardly pray,
For when we scarce can lift our voice
God is not far away.
A man should keep his vow when friends
Their vows are freely breaking,
And he will know God's peace within
When coward hearts are breaking.
A man should be courageous when
His fears beg him to quit,
For heroes aren't exempt from fear
But strive in spite of it.

IF YOU COULD LIFT THE MASK

When you see a broad-shouldered guy
Admired by boys and men,
Remember he may be hiding
Some bitter struggle within.
And friends we sometimes most admire
For their high station in life
May be battling grief unbearable
By singing through the strife
Remember when you see one smiling
And bravely facing tomorrow,
You'd see, if you could lift his mask,
Sometimes the face of sorrow.

Be strong, and let your heart take courage, all you
who wait for the Lord!   **Psalms 31:24**

Honor and Honesty

Character is what you are in the dark.

Dwight Moody

NO VACANCY

Oh God, give me a heart
As great as earth is great;
Yet let in me be found
No room to harbor hate.
Oh God, give me a mind
Vast as this universe;
Yet let there be in me
No room, one grudge to nurse.
Dear God, give me a soul
As spacious as the skies;
Yet may there be in me
No room to shelter lies.

Character is what God thinks of you. Reputation is what men think of you.

NO REGRETS! NO REMORSE!

I'd live in such a way
That in life's final test,
I can look back and say,
"I did my very best."
I'd live so true that friends
My life will quick endorse,
But most I'd like to live
Exempt from all remorse.
I'd live so wisely here
That were life's end to bring
A chance to turn back time,
I wouldn't change one thing.

Hypocrisy lies not in what you say to a person but what you think of him.   —Frank Rooney

THE INNER MAN

When people oft inquire,
"How do you feel today?"
I always say, "Just great,"
And that is all I say.
You see, I know my friends
Don't want a health report;
That's why I say I'm fine
In laughter and in sport.
And though I always say,
"Just great," so all can hear it,
I doubt if friends suspect
I'm speaking of my spirit.

KEEP YOUR SENSE OF HUMOR

Be this my glory and my crown,
"Life never made me mad,"
Nor did I let it get me down
Though sometimes I was sad.
When others raged at fate and chance
Indulging in self-pity,
I cancelled moods of desperate days
By being brave and witty.
And while friends let life anger them
On back-set days and fearful,
I'm proud life did not get me down
But left me brave and cheerful.

To those who by patience in well-doing seek for glory and honor and immortality, he will give eternal life.   **Romans 2:7**

Hypocrisy and Hospitality

Is it not heartening to see some pilgrim who is broken in body but who retains the unbroken splendor of an unbroken patience?

J. H. Jowett

NO MAN'S ENEMY

It was a happy day
When I realized the fact
That though one should hate me
I need not hate him back.
Or if some enemy
Should stoop to curse my name,
I do not have to stoop
To curse and act and blame.
If foes strike me today
Or on some future date,
I can love them instead.
No one can make me hate.

The noblest revenge is to forgive.

—Thomas Fuller

THE SECRET OF HAPPINESS

Abiding joy and peace
Come to a chosen lot
Who learn it only comes
To those who seek it not.
They learn it's never found
In glamourous undertakings,
Or in exploits of fame,
Or in headlines we're making.
Such joy and peace results
From serving God and others
And treating all men fair
And loving them as brothers.

PUTTING BACK THE STARS

May friends remember me
As one who with his light
Lit every lamp he saw
While stumbling through this night;
As one who gladly did
A thousand thankless chores
'Til those shut out from love
Could pass through long-locked doors.
May friends remember me
And say of my replies,
"His words put back the stars
In our dark, faithless skies."

IF I WERE KIND

God knows indeed how much
I loved my family here,
And yet within these walls
I hurt my loved ones dear.
For oft with words I crush
The ones I love the best,
And then speak gently to
Some strange or cherished guest.
I wish I were as kind
To those who love me so
As I appear to be
To those I hardly know.

So you also outwardly appear righteous to men, but within you are full of hypocrisy and iniquity.
Matthew 23:28

Important Ideals

Life is something that happens to us while we are making other plans.

Too low they build who build beneath the stars.

THE COMING OF THE DAWN

Death is not snuffing out life's flame
Precipitating strife;
It's like the first faint flush of dawn
Prophesying life.
And death is not some dead-end street
Where life abruptly ends;
It is a door that leads to realms
Where fairer life begins.
Death is not endless wandering
Like trails the nomads trod;
It is the surest road to life,
The nearer path to God.
And death is not some dark ordeal
Necessitating fear,
For it's as calm as peaceful sleep
In arms of someone dear.

SPEAK SOFTLY

To leave harsh words unspoken
Which we're inclined to say
Will leave some heart unbroken
And brighten someone's day.
To leave harsh words unspoken
Though they seem justified
Will impart faith and hope
To one who's lost his pride.
To leave harsh words unspoken
May cause some feud to end
And pave a path of peace
Where friendship starts again.

GO GET THEM BACK

Don't let your dreams take flight
For everybody knows
Dreams are the stuff from which
Great deeds and goodness flows.
Don't let your dreams take flight
Or let one dream grow cold,
For when your dreams have died
You've precondemned your soul.
Don't let your dreams take flight.
Losing one dream is sin;
And if your dreams have fled
Go get them back again.

God has no larger field for the man who is not faithfully doing his work where he is.

STRANGE VISITOR

When I saw his kind face
I opened wide my door
And asked the stranger in
Thinking we'd met before.
We sat and talked all day
Of brave exploits he's done,
Of fame and wealth he'd gained,
Of battles fought and won.
Admiring him I asked,
"Don't I know you, good friend?"
"You should," he wept. "I am
The man you might have been."

*Surely the righteous shall give thanks to thy name;
the upright shall dwell in thy presence.*

Psalms 140:13

Impressive Ideas

*Some churchmembers have faces long enough to
make a mule jealous.*

A retentive memory may be a good thing but
there is something to be said for the ability to
forget.

Refusing to go to church where hypocrites were,
he eventually went to hell to spend an eternity
with them.

SILENT WAYS

It comforts me when I recall
How quietly turns this earthly ball,
For 'midst the noise of man-made violence
God does his work in perfect silence.
How silently sunrises come
And night slips in serenely dumb.
Springtime tiptoes as if it feared
One soul should know when it appeared.
And since quiet work brings God high praise,
We too must work in silent ways.

Men possess thoughts but ideas possess men.
—Max Lerner

UNWELCOME GALILEAN

At our church door a man appeared
Whose skin was dark, whose clothes were weird.
He was not black; he was not white
And so I blocked his path that night.
And as he turned I saw the Man
Had unhealed wounds in distraught hands.
How could I know He was in town?
Who would have dreamed He was that brown?

THE PATIENT GOD

In history books you'll learn
The God who formed the earth
Has never with His hands
Constructed one small church,
Or built one school or house
With His almighty arms
Or spanned one mountain gorge
Or plowed the fertile farms.
God doesn't work that way
Although He's good and great.
He's left some work for us
And He's prepared to wait.

THREE CROSSES

They killed the Nazarene
Because He was so good;
They crucified the thieves
Because they were no good.
Men still scorn culprits weird
As noonday scorns the night,
And folk too good are feared
As darkness fears the light.

Everyone says forgiveness is a lovely idea, until
they have something to forgive.
—C. S. Lewis

There is nothing quite so powerful in the world
as an idea whose time has come.
—Victor Hugo

*How great are thy works, O Lord! Thy thoughts
are very deep!* **Psalms 92:5**

Inequities and Injustice

In the little world in which children have their existence, whosoever brings them up, there is nothing so finely perceived and so finely felt as injustice.　　　**Charles Dickens**

Jesus taught us not only to love our enemies but also to treat our friends a little better.

LET NONE STOOP SO LOW

When he speaks ill of others
And shreds them right and left,
He doesn't suspect we know
He's bragging on himself.
Yet words of gossip kill
Without pain or compunction
To him who does the killing;
That's how a gossip functions.
Then let none stoop so low
To speak ill words of others,
If in promoting self
We have to hurt our brothers.

WE'D LAUGH

If Christ should come once more
To live among us men,
I think we'd treat Him kinder
Than Pharisees back then.
I think we'd ask Him home,
Inviting Him for dinner,
And treat Him like a guest
Instead of some vile sinner.
We're much more civil now.
Yet soon as we were fed
We'd talk 'til He departed,
Then laugh at what He said.

IF YOU'LL ONLY LISTEN

In November please remember
When the weather grows chilled,
Many poor children starve
Shivering and ill.
In December please remember
When lights of Christmas glisten,
Children can be heard crying
If you'll only listen.

Watch any child at play. While adult beholders scurry around for happiness, the child holds it carelessly in his hands.

　　　　　　　　　　　　—Morris Longstreth

PEOPLE NEED PRAISE

If at my door I struck
Some beggar's body frail,
I think the law should come
And cart me off to jail.
Yet there's no law against
My crushing someone's mind,
Or letting one starve for
Praises sincere and kind.
Yet praise we oft withhold
From some deserving friend
Is ten times worse, I think,
Than striking beggar men.

Man's capacity for Justice makes democracy possible, but man's inclination to injustice makes democracy necessary.　　　—Reinhold Niebuhr

For I the Lord love justice, I hate robbery and wrong.　　　　　　　　　**Isaiah 61:8**

f you will be kind to this people and please them, and speak good words to them, then they will be your servants for ever.
2 Chronicles 10:7

SPEAK EVIL OF NO ONE

Banish words of strife
And every unkind word;
Squelch scandals cruel and mean
Nor tell what you have heard.
Crush with your will and mind
Gossip so uncouth,
Expelling from your thoughts
Falsehoods half mixed with truth.
Commit to silent tombs
All rumors false and true,
And then you need not fear
What friends may say of you

Hear, for I will speak noble things, and from my lips will come what is right. **Proverbs 8:6**

Inspiring Individuals

Train up a child in the way he should go . . .
and go that way yourself.

CHILDREN ARE MESSENGERS

His childish words move me
And probe me to the depth
Each time I hear him say,
"I'm walking in your steps."
His thoughts stab me awake
And in my heart ring true
Each time he says, "Daddy,
I plans to be like you."
His prayers convince me so
Of being harsh and petty
Each time I hear him pray,
"God, make me good like Daddy."
How strange that God conveys
Through lips of tender youth,
Heaven's profoundest thoughts
And earth's sublimest truth.

PICKING UP GLASS

Each day a small oil can
He took where'er he went,
And silenced things that squeaked
And never charged a cent.
If in his path he found
Some bits of broken glass,
He picked them up, so girls
And barefoot boys could pass.
Most folk just laughed at him
And yet those golden deeds
Have preached more faith to me
Than all the ancient creeds.

People have no right to make fools of themselves,
unless they have no relations to blush for them.
—Thomas Haliburton

SPEAK UP WITH COURAGE

When Martin Luther cried,
"God help me, Here I stand!"
He struck a note for freedom
That rung across the land.
When brave Columbus roared
To mutiny-minded seamen,
"Sail on! I say, sail on!"
He rang the bell of freedom.
When Patrick Henry shouted,
"Give me liberty or death,"
He strengthened freedom's cause
With that courageous breath.
When brave MacArthur wept
And vowed, "I will return,"
He wrote a page for freedom
Which all the world must learn.
Since freedom is never free
Let us say when discouraged,
"As millions have died for freedom
Let us speak up with courage."

There are only two lasting bequests we can **ever**
hope to give our children. One of these is roots;
the other, wings.

"A disciple is not above his teacher, nor a servant
above his master; it is enough for the disciple to
be like his teacher, and the servant like his mas-
ter." **Matthew 10:24**

Joy in Jesus

All history is incomprehensible without Christ.
Ernest Renan

TAKE UP YOUR CROSS

I said, "You ask too much!
A fellow has to live;
Still You come begging me
To give and give and give."
"And do I ask too much?
And does one have to live?
I had to die," He wept,
"And pray, 'Forgive, forgive.' "

Jesus Christ, the condescension of divinity, and the exaltation of humanity.   —Phillips Brooks

NEW CALVARIES

In sacred Galilee
And holy Palestine
Christ made the blind to see
And water blushed to wine.
He raised the dead to life
And lame men found release,
And even on a cross
He gave an outcast peace.
Today, new crosses call
And we new Calvaries climb,
That we might bless our world
As Christ blessed Palestine.

You may go the world over, and you will not find a single believer who is disappointed in the once crucified, now glorified, soon coming King. This is the best answer to the skepticism of the day. Take any class of society, the highest or the lowest, and there is not an instance of one who trusted in the Lord and was confounded.
—William Pennefeather

The religion that makes a man look sick certainly won't cure the world.

WHERE'ER HIS SHADOW FALLS

Where'er His shadow fell
Became a sacred place,
And bread He touched and blessed
Possessed a sweeter taste.
He made the deaf to hear,
The lame leaped with surprise,
Lepers He touched were cleansed
And He healed sightless eyes.
Today all bread is sweet
Blessed by the Meek and Lowly;
Where'er His shadow falls
In all of earth, seems holy.

But grow in the grace and knowledge of our Lord and Savior Jesus Christ.   **2 Peter 3:18**

Juveniles and Jobs

If this government is ever demoralized, it will come from trying to live without work.

Abraham Lincoln

CHURCH WORK

The nicest words I've ever heard
Came when my preacher asked,
"For Jesus and His church would you
Perform a special task?"
Surprise my church should think of me,
I said that I would do it,
Especially since I'd craved church work
Though not a person knew it.
Through all these years that memory shines
And means so very much—
The day the preacher gave to me
A special task at church.

The fellow who pulls the oars seldom has time to rock the boat.

THE REAL ISSUE

It's not, "What did you do
With tough breaks and paths blocked?"
The question is what did you do
When opportunity knocked?
It's not whether or not
Curve balls were thrown at you;
The question is, "When strikes whizzed past
What did you bravely do?"
It's not, "Were you shortchanged
Of talents when you started?"
But what have you been doing
With talents God imparted?

Other people can't make you see with their eyes.
They can only encourage you to use your own.

CONTENTMENT FROM SERVING

If you would find contentment
One law must be observed,
You can't live life self-centered.
Each man is born to serve.
And dreaming of self-glory
One finally finds his schemes
Of self-exalting turn
Into nightmarish dreams.
Contentment comes from serving
And joy from deep self-giving,
And no shortcut is known
To happy, joyful living.

THE TASK

When least prepared to choose,
Young people have to choose
How they will live their lives
And how their talents use.
So young and tender they,
So grave the choices given,
Yet youth so unprepared
Choose lives of hell or heaven.
All questions they must answer
Which life is sure to ask;
How strange when least prepared,
God gives the hardest task.

Do not be conformed to this world but be transformed by the renewal of your mind, that you may prove what is the will of God, what is good and acceptable and perfect. **Romans 12:2**

Keys to Knowledge

**Knowledge and timber should not be much used
until they are seasoned.**

Oliver Wendell Holmes

Some people know a lot more when you try to tell them something than when you ask them something.

KNOW WHERE YOU'RE GOING

The world will make a place for you
If you know where you're going;
They'll stand aside and help you pass
If you'll just keep on growing.
But they will hold you in contempt
And scorn your lofty morals
If they discover you're content
To rest upon your laurels.
The world takes pride in goals you've won
And has from your beginning.
But they'll admire you so much more
If you'll go right on winning.
But if you rest content and cease
When others are aspiring,
Friends will begrudge you air to breathe
Nor weep when you are dying.
For we expect exploits from you
And hope you will be giving
The best you have and all you have
In brave adventurous living.
But if you give your second best
You'll reap what you are sowing,
While we stand up and cheer those on
Who know where they are going.

Knowledge humbles the great man, astonishes the common man, puffs up the little man.

Knowledge is awareness that fire will burn; wisdom is remembering the blister.

THANK GOD FOR DISCONTENT

To graduate excites in me
A most unusual pride,
And yet surprisingly I find
I'm still unsatisfied.
I've barely scratched the surface of
Rich wisdom unconcealed,
And now I'm destined to seek on
Until all truth's revealed.
Perhaps I'm standing on truth's shores
Clutching one shiny stone;
Perhaps disquietude I feel
Is thirst for truth unknown.
What if from this commencement hour
Until Truth's Kingdom comes,
I must in ranks of discontent
Keep step with distant drums?
What if unrest I feel today
Is something God has sent?
I think it's heaven's choicest gift.
Thank God for discontent.

It's what you learn after you know it all that counts.
—William Griffin

For the Lord is a God of knowledge.

1 Samuel 2:3

Kindness to Kinsman

It is necessary to be almost a genius to make a good husband. — Honoré de Balzac

I'VE BEEN BLEST INDEED

You've been an ideal wife
And that's why I love you;
Your sermon is your life
And every part is true
You've been an ideal wife
Whose words and deeds have shown
A love for God and friends
Which very few have known.
God smiled on me and gave
To me an ideal wife,
And I've been blest indeed;
Your life inspires my life.

Love doesn't consist in gazing at each other but in looking outward together in the same direction.

FOR OUR CHILDREN'S SAKE

God bless us married folk!
We have so much at stake,
And we could lose it all
By just one small mistake.
But we have much to win
If we bear our mild yoke
And so we plead in prayer,
"God bless us married folk.
Fill us with love and faith
Lest we one heart should break,
And bless us married folk
For our sweet children's sake."

THE BEST GIFT

Her steps are slowing down,
Her strength is nearly gone
And chances are she may
Not be with us too long.
Of course that makes me sad
But I rejoice to know
That Mother is prepared
And unafraid to go.
She's lived a life of faith
And all her works abide,
So why should I begrudge
Her rest at eventide.
Yet I oft ask myself,
"What can a child present
To make these days her best,
Lest she feel discontent?"
Of gifts a mother craves
There's one above all other,
And I will give it now,
"I dearly love you, Mother."

MY CHILDREN

I loved them so when they were small
And kissed each bruise when they would fall
Their childish feet as day would close
Ofttimes would stand upon my toes.
Around me now no children play,
No feet walk on my toes today.
For since they're grown and live apart,
They only walk upon my heart.

Do all things without grumbling or questioning, that you may be blameless and innocent. — **Philippians 2:14, 15**

Kneeling and Knowing

Groanings which cannot be uttered are often prayers which cannot be refused.
Charles H. Spurgeon

GOD COMES AT EVENTIDE

If I when day concludes
Have not failed in my duty
Nor uttered unkind words
Or closed my eyes to beauty,
And if I with my strength
Have done my daily labor
Without complaint or fuss
And if I've loved my neighbor,
Then I when day concludes
Musing by glowing embers
Will drink the cup of peace
That comes when one remembers:
"When one has done his best
God comes at eventide
To be a special Guest
Around that man's fireside."

The secret of prayer is prayer in secret.

PAUL'S SECRET

In prison dark he wrote
When eyes could hardly see,
"I can do all things through
The Lord who strengthens me."
I asked, "How could one plagued
Write words of faith like those,
Who oft was bound with chains
And garbed in prison clothes?"
The secret came to me
When one verse I received,
"To live is Christ," Paul said.
"I know whom I've believed."

He who prays without confidence cannot hope that his prayers will be answered.

FERVENT PRAYER

It's not the eloquence
With which a prayer begins,
Nor piety of the voice
That makes a prayer ascend.
It's not how long we pray
Or prayers deep and reflective,
Nor is it kneeling down
That makes a prayer effective.
It's earnestness that counts,
Not eloquence of speech;
God loves a fervent prayer;
Such prayers to heaven reach.

A BRIGHT OUTLOOK

If e'er your outlook's dark
As on a starless night,
Just lift your eyes to God;
The uplook's very bright.
And though Satan succeeds
In hedging you about,
He cannot roof you in
Or shut the Lord Christ out.
Your future is as bright
As truth within God's book,
And when your outlook's dark,
Try then the upward look.

Kneeling down on the beach we prayed.
Acts 21:5

Learning to Live

We must make up for the threatened brevity of
life by heightening the intensity of life.

Joshua Liebman

PEOPLE ARE LIKE TREES

Tall trees sometimes
When storms are lashing,
Groan and surprise us
When we see them crashing.
Those who ask, "Why?"
Usually learn the truth:
They're rotten inside
Or lack deep roots.

Too often a man handles life as he does bad
weather. He whiles away the time as he waits
for it to stop.   —Alfred Polger

LIFE IS UPHILL

Life is mostly uphill
And people must accept it;
Yet some think God's plan failed,
Like He could not have helped it.
He planned this path so steep
And I am glad He planned it;
That's why we give our best—
An uphill life demands it.
And of this climbing urge,
Life only satisfies it;
So uphill paths are blest,
And there's no use denying it.

Life is a grindstone; whether it grinds you down
or polishes you up depends on what you're made
of.

Life lets us make something for ourselves or
something of ourselves.

MY BEGINNING

Today is to my past
A day of ending,
But to the rest of my life,
Today is the beginning.
What though my past is marred,
Or my task unfinished?
Today I'll start all over
With a future unblemished.
Today I'll change my pace
From failure to winning,
Because to the rest of my life,
Today is my beginning.

TALKING TO THE SHEPHERD

Insomniac I am,
Have learned the key to sleep
Is talking to my Shepherd
Instead of counting sheep.
For oft in telling Jesus
My fears and doubts and woes
I've found to my delight
My sleepless eyes soon close.
Why should I count sheep now
When sleepless hours mock?
I've learned to count my blessings
And with my Shepherd talk.

I came that they may have life, and have it abun-
dantly.   **John 10:10**

Life's Lessons

There is a great deal of human nature in people.
Mark Twain

STANDING UP TO LIFE

Don't run away and hide
From troubles that you see.
You'll multiply the woes
From which you try to flee.
We ought to meet our troubles
Head-on and unafraid;
It makes our courage grow
And helps our fears to fade.
And if we dauntless face
The frightful, dreaded foe,
We'll find by being brave
Our courage starts to grow;
And soon discover, too,
By standing up to life
That every trouble conquered
Equips for future strife.
Yet if you should forget
And fearful run away,
You'll find, unsolved, each woe
Will seek you out one day.

FAITH TO MOVE A HILL

Great faith to move a mountain
Would surely give a thrill,
But I'd be glad to have
A faith to move some hills.
For hills have slowed me down,
And things I cannot master;
And faith must move them, surely,
If I move forward faster.
Lord, let saints move their mountains!
The one thing that I'm needing
Is faith to deal with hills
That keep me from succeeding.

There are no hopeless situations; there are only
men who have grown hopeless about them.
—Clare Booth Luce

BEAUTY, ART AND PLEASURE

I thought life should consist
Of mostly art and pleasure,
But life gave sorrow's cup
And I drank without measure.
I thought life should consist
Of mostly art and beauty,
But life gave work and sweat
And I found life was duty.
Yet duty's rich reward
And sorrow's rarest treasure,
I've learned through toil and tears,
Are beauty, art, and pleasure.

WHO WEARS MY HAT

Instead of blaming others
For woes our lives impart
We ought to look nearby,
Perhaps within our hearts.
For if one thought things through
He may discover that
The man who plagues him most
Is he who wears his hat.
And I, if I should kick
The man who blights my ways—
I'd be incapable
Of sitting down for days.

Let all things be done for edification. **1 Corinthians 14:26**

Living Loyally

The great use of life is to spend it for something that will outlast it.   **William James**

A NAME KNOWN TO GOD

I searched the world to find
Earth's most heroic name;
I scanned thick history books;
I probed vast halls of fame.
I pondered martyrs buried
Beneath church spires and steeples;
I wept by shrines of freedom
Where patriots died for people.
I searched until I found
A fact revealed to few:
The true and great heroes,
Historians never knew
Unpraised, most heroes lived
And oft laid down their lives
With none to note their deeds
Of bravery facing strife.
None knew the wounds they bore,
For brave men don't complain;
No markers mark their graves
And no one knows their names.
Yet I think God takes note
Of those who without praise,
Stood at their post of duty
And struggled through life's days.
I searched and found the bravest,
At least most all of them,
Possessed names known to God
And only known to Him.

REMORSE

With heart sincere and steady stroke
I carved my name upon an oak.
'Twas then I vowed to keep my name
Untarnished and exempt from shame.
But as years passed I then realized
My vow to God was compromised.
Yet every promise that I broke
Still haunts me when I pass that oak.

KIDS NEED BOTH PARENTS

In suit for their divorce,
They nor the judge could smile,
For both sought custody
Of their one cherished child.
"You both deserve the child,"
The kindly judge replied,
"And since the lad is here
We'll let him now decide."
He said, "Son, you must choose
The parent you prefer";
The boy cried innocently,
"Oh, I'll take both, kind sir."
Through this they saw themselves
As vain and cruel, of course;
And they were so ashamed
They cancelled their divorce.

It is a funny thing about life; if you refuse to accept anything but the best, you very often get it.
     —Somerset Maugham

Those who devise good meet loyalty and faithfulness.   **Proverbs 14:22**

Love and Longevity

Let God have your life; He can do more with it than you can.   **Dwight L. Moody**

SIXTY YEARS OF GRACE

An artist made a portrait
Of one forlorn of youth,
Yet wrinkles in her face
Were lines of love and truth.
As she left, a young girl asked,
"What reason or what rhyme
Should make one so wrinkled
Use up an artist's time?"
The artist scanned the critic
But saw unkindness there
Though she was young and tender
And very, very fair.
He smiled, "We artists see
A beauty hid to eyes;
Her face revealed God's love
A kindness I admire.
Surely the Master-Artist
Through sixty years of grace,
Has made a masterpiece
Of that dear lady's face."

Winter is on my head but eternal spring is in my heart; I breathe at this hour the fragrance of the lilacs, the violets and the roses, just as twenty years ago. The nearer I approach the end, the plainer I hear around the immortal symphonies of the worlds which invite me.

—Victor Hugo

The most consummately beautiful thing in the universe is the rightly fashioned life of a good person.   —George H. Palmer

YOUR HEART IS TRUE

A thousand ways I've proven you
And I have found your heart is true.
I must admit I now aspire
To be like you whom I admire.
You are to me exhibit "A"
Of what I'd like to be someday.

SO LET ME DIE IN FAITH

My body weary from these years
Will to the earth return,
But my soul freed from flesh will soar
To God for whom I yearn.
And friends will do me wrong to say
I'm buried in a tomb
Or weep beside my grave not knowing
I'm in my Father's room.
Set free by death, my soul can't be
Imprisoned in a grave;
When breath expires my soul will fly
Back to the God who gave.
What seems like death to fearful men,
Let me reach to embrace,
Convinced that Christ will be there waiting
So let me die in faith!

Life is not something to be salvaged. It is an investment to be used in the world.

A good man obtains favor from the Lord.
Proverbs 12:2

Lust for Liberty

Only a virtuous people can be free. Freedom can survive only if the people are inwardly governed by a moral law. **John Courtney Murray**

We have learned to fly through the air like birds and to swim through the sea like fish. When will we learn to walk the earth like men?

BETTER MEN

Lord, we need better towns
With better homes and schools,
And we need better states
With better laws and rules.
Lord, we need better jobs
With higher scales of pay,
But more than all of these
We need one thing today.
Lord, give us better men
With Christlike minds and souls,
And then without a doubt
We'll win these higher goals.

WORLD CHANGERS

You say you'd change the world
If you could have your way;
Well, I dislike it too
The way it is today.
I'd like to have a world
Exempt from war and fear,
But come to think of it,
Maybe that's why we're here.
Perhaps God bids us change
The world from what it is,
Nor be content with it
Until it looks like His.

THE PROUDEST OF THE PROUD

Some mock the flag I love
And its true claims dismiss;
Yet I'll not be ashamed
Of such a flag as this.
Nor do I blush to say
A lump comes in my throat
When on a staff or pole
I see Old Glory float.
And when my flag goes by,
Though I'm lost in the crowd,
Yet in my heart I am
The proudest of the proud.

The best reformers are those who commence on themselves.

AS GOOD AS TRUTH

Love America? You bet!
Pray tell, why not?
Can you tell me where there's
A fairer spot?
Love America? I'll say!
Can one do less?
And then in prayer ask God
His land to bless?
Love America? Indeed.
And I from tender youth
Have loved her next to God
And good as truth.

For freedom Christ has set us free; stand fast therefore, and do not submit again to a yoke of slavery. **Galatians 5:1**

Remember not the sins of my youth, or my transgressions; according to thy steadfast love remember me. **Psalms 25:7**

BUYING MEMORIES

Extravagant spending
May seem a bit distasteful,
But if it buys a memory
Such spending is not wasteful.
And every purchased rose
Leaves memories sweet to cherish,
And fragrance of memories cling
Long after roses perish.
Love is a spendthrift thing—
Giving, always giving,
And wise is he who buys
Some memories worth reliving.

I remember the days of old, I meditate on all that thou hast done. **Psalms 143:5**

Meditation on Mothers

Mother is the name for God in the lips and hearts
of little children. **William M. Thackeray**

A mother is not a person to lean on but a person
to make leaning unnecessary.

—Dorothy Fisher

A MOTHER'S LOVE

A mother's love is strong
And it always abides
With such intensity
'Til life is made worthwhile.
And never once have I
Amidst triumph or strife
Questioned my mother's love
Through changing years of life.
I think a mother's love
Like priceless art appears,
Growing in elegance
With all the passing years.

SOMEBODY'S MOTHER

Somebody's mother today
Will linger by her phone
Hoping one child will call
Before the day has flown.
Somebody's mother will weep,
Heartbroken and stunned tonight,
Because her children gone
Forgot to call or write.
Somebody's mother somewhere
Will kiss with lips of grief,
Portraits of children grown
And cry herself to sleep.

I KNOW NOW

My mother never slept
No matter where we'd been
Until she knew for sure
Her children were all in.
We'd beg her not to wait
But she could not refrain,
And when we asked her, "Why?"
She never could explain.
But since I have some girls
And sons as tall as men,
I know how Mother felt
Until we all came in.

TOO LATE

I wonder why we fail
To speak that loving word
To those we love the best,
To those who've seldom heard?
It's not that we intend
To be the least unkind;
It's just that we neglect
Or let it slip our mind.
How sad to think we'll wait
'Til friends have passed away,
And then, too late, speak thoughts
We should have said today.

To a man who has had a Christian mother, all
women are sacred for her sake.

—Jean Paul Richter

Let your father and mother be glad, let her who
bore you rejoice. **Proverbs 23:25**

Memorable Moments

God has given us memory that we might have roses in December.　　　**James Barrie**

THESE THINGS I'VE LOVED

I've loved the hills of home,
And on their lofty heights
I've heard daybreak and seen
The day embrace the night.
I've loved the restless tide
Reclining on the shore,
Awaiting dawn to come
To leave with thunderous roar.
I've loved the thunder clap
And lightning in the storm,
And at my window smiled
To see my God perform.

A good thing to have up your sleeve is a funny bone.

CLOSED CHAPTERS

When he marched off to school
I knew I had no choice,
But afterthoughts left me
Unable to rejoice.
And though I kissed his cheek,
Yet how could I be glad?
For he was only six—
The last small child I had.
'Twas then I sensed somehow,
As I waved to my son,
A chapter in life's book
For me was nearly done.

It's a wonderful generation to belong to. Everything that's wrong is the fault of the generation ahead of us and is going to have to be corrected by the one after us.　　　—Bill Vaughan

PRESCRIPTION FOR SELF-PITY

From life's inequities
I pitied my poor self,
But all self-pity fled
When I saw one born deaf.
I wept because I had
To wear eyeglasses thick,
But when a blind man passed
I felt ashamed and sick.
I crippled on a crutch
And grieved from night 'til dawn,
But weeping ceased when I
Saw one with both legs gone.

Some people bring happiness wherever they go; others whenever they go.

The memory of the righteous is a blessing.
Proverbs 10:7

Mirth of Marriage

Try praising your wife, even if it does frighten her at first. **Billy Sunday**

Success in love consists not so much in marrying the one person who can make you happy as in escaping the many who could make you miserable.

The secret of happy marriage is simple; just keep on being as polite to each other as you are to your best friends. —Robert Quillen

WHAT GOD HATH JOINED

Some live together though
They're never joined in heart,
While others bound by love
Are forced to live apart.
Some whisper marriage vows
But are not wed in mind;
Some voice no vows and yet
They're bound by love's sweet sign.

THE HOME WE LOVE

We need great homes of love
Where parents understand
The needs of every child
And guide with gentle hands;
Great homes where love forgives
If one should cross the path
Of someone innocent;
Kind homes devoid of wrath;
And where each child obeys
Nor feels misunderstood:
God give us greater homes
With parents kind and good.

To disagree without being disagreeable is a winsome trait, worthy of royalty and quite becoming to the true diplomat and noblest gentlemen.

WE'VE SEEN OUR BRAVE PARENTS

Let us so live our lives
In these dark desperate days
That children in our homes
Will sense we're strong and brave.
Let us conduct ourselves
On this and every day
In such courageous fashion
'Til children of us say,
"God matched us with the future
And made us fearless of it,
For we've seen our brave parents
Face their trouble and solve it."

CHANGELESS LOVE

I'll love you in success
When you've achieved your goal,
But I'll not love you less
When you are ill and old.
I'll love you when you're young
With face and form approved,
But I'll love deeper still
When beauty is removed.
For I have pondered well
Just what true friendship means;
My changeless love I give
Unchanged through changing scenes.

Let marriage be held in honor among all.
Hebrews 13:4

My Master

There is not a heart but has its moments of long-ing, yearning for something better, nobler, holier than it knows now.   **Henry Ward Beecher**

HIS CALLOUSED KNEES

I love the Nazareth youth
And trust the virgin-born;
I love Christ of the cross,
The Lord of Easter morn.
But Jesus washing feet
I've loved the best and shall,
And how could one refuse
Christ girded with a towel?
And you will love Him, too,
If e'er He walks your street,
And you'll know Him by knees,
Calloused from washing feet.

LOVE MUST SUFFER

To sense God's heart is crushed
Whenever His people suffer
Makes it less hard for me
To be His worshipper.
For I could not love God
Were He too harsh to care,
Or else insensitive
To heavy loads I bear.
Yet Calvary reoccurs
As when Christ was forsaken,
And as His heart broke once
So it's been always breaking.

The way to love anything is to realize that it may be lost.   —G. K. Chesterton

Someday, after mastering the winds, the waves, the tides, and gravity, we shall harness for God the energies of love, and then, for the second time in the history of the world man will dis-cover fire.   —Teilhard de Chardin

YET I THINK MARY WEPT

Who would have ever guessed
The God who made the world
Would one day enter it
Born of a peasant girl?
And that upon her breast
The God who reigns above
Would there enrobed in flesh
Reveal the Father's love?
Yet I think Mary wept
When flames of candles tossed
Rude shadows in the stall—
And she could see a cross.

IT WAS YOU

Who nailed Him high against the sky?
Who watched Him die as He prayed, "Why?"
It was I! It was I! It was I!
Who hung the Jew in public view
And bruised Him blue and cursed Him too?
It was you! It was you! It was you!
Who mocked His plea, when on the tree
As blood flowed free, He prayed for me?
It was I! It was you! It was we!

For you have one master, the Christ.
Matthew 23:10

Nearness to Nature

The landscape belongs to the men who look at it.
Ralph Waldo Emerson

It is well to stop our star gazing occasionally and consider the ground under our feet. Maybe it is celestial, too; maybe this brown, sun-tanned, sin-stained earth is a sister to the morning and the evening star. —John Burroughs

HOW CAN WE HELP OTHERS

If you should find a larva
Bursting its cocoon this spring,
For goodness sake don't assist it.
Don't touch the struggling thing.
For our assistance weakens them until
They're incapable of surviving,
If freed or partially freed,
Except by their own striving.
But they will, if unassisted,
After struggling free, arise
On wings made strong by struggle
And become butterflies.
God, how can we help others
Without their soon relinquishing
Their striving to free themselves
So essential for strengthening?

If God had been here last summer and had seen some things I saw, I am sure He would have thought this upper heaven superfluous.
—Emily Dickinson

MOUNTAIN MEN

The finest wood that's known
To make a violin
Is carved from mountain trees,
Grown where the air is thin.
For music that exudes
From such violins, we know,
Is lofty as tall peaks,
And sweet as purest snow.
As it is true of trees
So it's with mountain men,
They grow in strength through storms
And facing lashing wind.
Let me, whipped by life's storms,
Pause daily to remember
That best violins are carved
From tested mountain timber.

THE MIRACLE OF SPRING

The naked trees all blush
When springtime comes to town,
And so in modesty
They slip on their new gown.
Birds harmonize as if
They were a vested choir,
Singing for royalty
'Neath some cathedral spire.
Can anyone explain
Or have the scholars found
What factors transform life
When springtime comes to town?

And out of the ground the Lord God made to grow every tree that is pleasant to the sight and good for food.   **Genesis 2:9**

Neglecting the Nazarene

Christianity is never escape. Christianity is always conquest.   **William Barclay**

WHEN CHRIST HAS BEEN REJECTED

When I pass by a run-down church
With doors and windows rotten,
I feel I'm looking at a church
Where love has been forgotten.
When I behold a broken home
Or some deserted child,
I feel I'm looking at a home
Where love and kindness died.
When I see one enslaved by sin,
Friendless and dejected,
I feel I'm looking at a life
Where Christ has been rejected.

NO HALFWAY HOUSE

Christ is the Lord of All
To all who bear His name,
Or He's not Lord at all
No matter what we claim.
For there's no halfway house
To truth and faith He brings;
We must give all to Him
If He's our King of Kings.
But we betray the Christ
And crucify anew
Until he's Lord of Lords
In all we say and do.

Religion is betting one's life there is a God.
—Donald Hankey

The trouble with us is that we have been inoculated with small doses of Christianity which keep us from catching the real thing.
—Leslie Weatherhead

IF JESUS CAME

If Jesus came to our small town,
He would not wear a robe or gown;
He would not have long hair or beard
Or dress Himself in sandals weird.
He would not have that ancient look
As He appears in picture book;
And if He ever stood to teach
We'd hear no accent in His speech.
I think He'd look like every man,
And seeing Him we'd understand
How if He came to our small town
The people here would turn Him down.
And is that not the reason why
The angry crowds cried, "Crucify!"
The reason they rejected Him
Was that He looked so much like them.
But down our streets as He once came
He comes to us and calls our names;
But we don't know Him in our town.
We wanted Him to wear a crown.

We will not neglect the house of our God.
Nehemiah 10:39

Neighbors Are Needed

Some people think they are generous because they give away free advice.

WHAT WILL I GET

In cruder days we sold
As slaves our darker brothers,
But we grew civilized
And more humane to others.
Yet auction blocks will prove
If any searcher delves,
Today, instead of slaves,
We merely sell our selves.

Superior people talk about ideas; average people talk about things; little people talk about other people.

ALMS GIVEN IN SECRET

I said, "It's one of those days
And I am quite relieved
That it is over with
For nothing was achieved."
God said, "But I saw you
When you so quietly placed
Coins in the hand of him
Who had a beggar's face.
And though earth's accolades
Bypass your deed and name,
Yet it's admitted you
To Heaven's Hall of Fame."

Most of today's troubles on which we stub our toes are the unpleasant, unperformed duties which we shoved aside yesterday.

Some people we click with, some folk we cross with. Love is manifest when we love those who cross us.　　　　　　—Ted Kummerfield

AS A STRANGER

Today a stranger attended church
But since none knew him,
And since we were busy worshiping,
Nobody welcomed him.
Coldhearted we came to church,
Coldhearted we left the same,
Ignoring the stranger completely;
Nobody knew his name.
"I missed Christ presence today,"
Tonight I cried;
He wept, "As a stranger I came today
But no one recognized."

The best part of a real-estate bargain is the neighbor.　　　　　　—Austin O'Malley

IF WE ONLY KNEW

If we knew tonight we had
Our last chance for decades
To see the stars displayed,
I think we'd gaze and gaze.
If we knew sight was failing
And soon we would be blind,
We'd gaze for days at beauty
And hold it in our minds.
If we knew today would be
Our last day of good health,
We'd spend it visiting friends,
Sharing affection we'd felt.

You shall not bear false witness against your neighbor.　　　　　　Exodus 20:16

Observations of Oldsters

A happy man or woman is a better thing to find than a five-pound note. He or she is a radiating focus of good will; and their entrance into a room is as though another candle had been lighted.
Robert Louis Stevenson

THE REAPING TIME

The harvest years are best
With deepest peace sublime,
For that is when we reap
The fruit of our lifetime.
The harvest years shine bright,
For in the reaping years
We can look back and read
The meaning of our tears.
Of course all have regrets;
Remorse is not a crime!
That is, if we'll let God
Forgive at reaping time.

MOST USEFUL SOULS BEAR SCARS

Beneath an apple tree
Boys standing on the ground
Reared back and threw their sticks,
Knocking apples down.
I saw each limb was scarred
From many a glancing blow,
For boys always throw things
At trees where apples grow.
Lush fruit on laden limbs
Thrown at by hands so youthful
Remind me of some friends;
Scars prove their lives were fruitful.

Death is not extinguishing the light; it is putting out the lamp because dawn has come.

WHERE GOD IS FOUND

God is more often found
Where hearts are crushed with grief
Than in cold stuffy churches
Where sermonettes are preached.
God is more likely known
Through lives of gentle people
Than through stain-glassed cathedrals
Adorned with cross-tipped steeple.
God is much clearer seen
Where souls with crosses falter
Than from new pews upholstered
Encircling ivory altars.

God is more anxious to forgive the blotted page of endeavor than the blank page of surrender.

SUNSET YEARS, SO-CALLED

If I in my old age
Can fill some useful spot,
Then I will not complain
If I am old or not,
If I in my old age
Can do some deed worthwhile
Then latter years will find
Me waiting with a smile.
If in the eve of life
I find these good surprises,
Then sunset years, so-called,
Will be to me sunrises.

The plowers plowed upon my back; they made long their furrows. **Psalms 129:3**

Obstacles and Opportunity

Success should not be measured by the height one attains, but by the obstacles one overcomes in their attainment. **Booker T. Washington**

A man should share the action and passion of his times at the peril of being judged not to have lived. —Oliver Wendell Holmes

HEARTBREAK AT DAWN

Exhibiting indifference
And displaying immunity
To the patient knocking
Of opportunity,
And even refusing
When hearing the knock,
To turn the key quickly
And unlock the lock,
Is the curse of today
And the heartbreak at dawn
To discover tomorrow—
Opportunity has gone.

HOW GOD WORKS

I begged my God to give
To me a sincere friend,
But He gave love and said,
"Each one His own must win."
I dreamed a dream and prayed
That world-wide strife would cease
But God touched my weak voice
And said, "You speak for peace."
When I prayed, "Smooth my path;
Replace my dingy hovel,"
God only gave me tools—
A hammer, saw and shovel.

GOD LOVES US AS WE ARE

You don't have to make home runs
When you stand up to bat;
Just try to get on first base
Or a little better than that.
You don't have to make it big
From your business earnings;
Just try to make a good living
And keep the home fires burning.
And you don't have to be famous
With a much-praised name;
Faithfulness in small things is better
Than making halls of fame.
If you can't be the sun or moon,
Settle for the evening star;
We don't have to prove our greatness.
God loves us as we are.

ABOUT LIFE

If mysteries of life were solved
It would challenge me not;
God never meant our life to be
With uncomplicated plot.
And lofty goals of life achieved
Some times means less than striving;
And so in life the journey counts
As much as mere arriving.
So life's impossibilities
More than success or ease,
Still challenge us and challenge best
To brave and nobler deeds.

Save me, O God! For the waters have come up to my neck. I sink in deep mire, where there is no foothold. **Psalms 69:1, 2.**

Optimistic Outlook

Happiness is a thing to be practiced daily like a violin.

Better keep yourself clean and bright: you are the window through which you must see the world. —George Bernard Shaw

ATTITUDE

Don't dare admit defeat
And you will surely see
How such an attitude
Insures a victory.
Don't dare admit you're beat
But hold the attitude
That victory will be reached,
And strength will be renewed.
Believe you cannot lose
And think young like a youth;
Then victory will be yours
As you blaze trails for truth.

WE CAN CONQUER DEATH

God has not promised
Us perfect health,
Glory and glamour,
Or limitless wealth.
God has not promised
Exemption from
Aches and agony
When illness comes.
But God has promised
His strength will brighten
Our golden years
When shadows lengthen.
And God has promised
Throughout life's days
Goodness and mercy
Shall follow always.

YOU CAN CHANGE THE WORLD

If you can walk with head held high
And look men squarely in the eye,
Nor stoop to steal or tell a lie,
Then you can change the world.
If you can sit with men condemned
Nor feel you are too good for them
But witness to His cross and Him,
Then you can change the world.
And with the love which Christ imparted
If you can rise when day has started
Stoop down to lift the broken-hearted,
Then you can change the world.

To live well we must have a faith fit to live by, a self fit to live with, and a work fit to live for. —Joseph Fort Newton

GREAT TIME TO BE ALIVE

Why talk of these tough times?
God matched our strength with them;
Can one evade his cross
And claim to follow Him?
Why criticize this age?
God's plan is not amiss;
God made us for tough times
To cope with days like this.
Why seek to flee from strife?
God plans for you to strive
In this the greatest age
Of all to be alive.

And now, my sons, listen to me: happy are those who keep my ways. **Proverbs 8:32**

Overcoming Opposition

With the soul that ever felt the sting of sorrow,
sorrow is a sacred thing. **William Cowper**

WHERE GOD'S BEST SOLDIERS LIVE

An ancient legend states
That of all soldiers known
No brave men can compare
With those from mountain homes.
For mountain men adapt
To each harsh soldier-task,
For they've grown up deprived
Along some highland pass.
So on affliction's mount
Some have found strength for life,
Proof that God's noblest oft
Come from highlands of strife.

BEST MARINERS

The best of skillful mariners,
So I've been told by friends,
Have been storm-tossed by waves,
And shipwrecked by the winds.
As storms teach skill to seamen
Where waves like mountains form,
So I, tossed on life's sea,
Have learned a lot through storm.
Lord, we who pray for peace,
But are to peace a stranger,
Dare not forget—best mariners
Acquired their skill through danger.

Judge a tree by its fruit, not its leaves.

—Phaedrus

PEARLS OF WISDOM

In ancient times they say
Pearl-divers were required
To cling to heavy rocks
And dive to depths desired.
They say gigantic stones
Would pull the diver down
So he could search and find
Where costly pearls were found.
Sometimes harsh loads in life,
Like stones, crush with despair
'Til we, submerged in troubles,
Find pearls of wisdom there.

ONLY THE GALLANT

None deserves success
Without a struggle,
And victory is sweetest
After a battle.
None deserves happiness
Who's lived unfaithful.
Only the gallant
Who strives uncomplaining
Deserves the victory
Of finding life's meaning.

When any calamity has been suffered, the first thing to be remembered, is, how much has been escaped. —Samuel Johnson

An unforgiving attitude and a grudge-bearing spirit are the weak pleasures of a little-hearted and narrow-minded people.

We had courage in our God to declare to you the
gospel of God in the face of great opposition.
1 Thessalonians 2:2

Pastor and People

Some ministers would make good martyrs; they are so dry they would burn well.

Charles Spurgeon

A SOUL CONVERTING STATION

Show me a church where people meet
And everyone is friendly,
And one where well-loved Scripture verses
Are quoted in sincerity;
And show to me a sanctuary
Where families bow on Sunday.
And where they leave to live that way
When they're at work on Monday;
And I'll show you a growing church,
And without hesitation
A church where lives are changed by Christ—
A soul-converting station.

PREACHING CAN SAVE THE DAY

Pulpits are so inept
And preachers' influence small
'Til critics often ask
What's the cause of it all.
Of course preachers get blamed
But let's give dogs their dues;
Powerless pulpits come
From prayerless, half-filled pews.
Pack all the churches full
Of Christians who can pray
And preaching will touch lives
And pulpits save the day.

A free people can be led a greater distance and to greater heights than a slave can be driven.

—David Sarnoff

To say what you mean without ever offending people is usually to say what you mean without making them believe you mean what you say.

—James Hilton

THE REAL ATHEISM

To affirm your faith
And quote the creed,
And then hate an enemy
Is atheism, indeed.
To attend church often
And then to turn
To doubt and worry
Is atheism confirmed.
To profess Christ's name
And go on cheating
Is not Christianity
But atheism succeeding.

THE CHRIST OF THE GHETTO

"It's awfully dark in here,"
I said to one confined;
"Are you not lonely here
And hungry half the time?"
Her answer startled me
As she lay on her bed;
"Could one be hungry here
When Jesus is his bread?
And though this little room
Is dark without a window,
God's love shines through each crack
And fills my room with splendor."

We are afflicted in every way, but not crushed; perplexed, but not driven to despair.

2 Corinthians 4:8

Persuasive Proclamation

Our chief want in life is somebody who shall make us do what we are capable of doing.

Carlyle

The essence of the minister lies in what God has created him to be rather than in what the church authorized him to do. —John Stacy

WINSOME PREACHING

When he first came to preach
With his ill-tutored witness,
We laughed behind his back
And many eyebrows lifted.
But when we saw his life
We didn't mind his speech;
We saw one living daily
The Gospel that he preached.
His words backed up with deeds
Won us through weeks of strife
From critics of the preacher
To witnesses for Christ.

WHY NOT PREACH ON

I said, "I'll preach no more,"
And one replied to me,
"Your task is very great.
Why quit the ministry?"
I cried, "I've paid my debt.
I tried to make earth better,
But things are getting worse
And I'm a deeper debtor."
He asked, "Why not preach on
And do all you know how?
Had you not preached these years
Earth would be worse than now."

A HOMETOWN WITNESS

Desiring to witness
I volunteered to preach,
But Jesus said to me,
"Go witness on your street."
"I seek a larger place,"
I pled in bold self-pity;
"Then go," He whispered low,
"Go witness in your city."
"I mean elsewhere," I begged,
"Like some far-distant place;
Lord, here in my hometown
They'd laugh right in my face."
He wept, "But Judea mocked;
Galilee turned me down;
Jerusalem spit on me;
They laughed in my hometown."
Deeply touched, I went forth
To witness to my neighbor
Who welcomed and made me glad
I dared to go and labor.
And I, surprised, soon learned
There are no distant places
With needs more deeply etched
Than on familiar faces.

Only once did God choose a completely sinless preacher. —Alexander Whyte

Go and proclaim in the hearing of Jerusalem, thus says the Lord.

Jeremiah 2:2

kept my faith, even when I said, "I am greatly afflicted."
Psalms 116:10

FAITH SUSPENDS A BRIDGE

Don't cross your rivers 'til you come
To where your rivers are,
For faith can make them disappear
And you will journey far.
For crossing rivers in one's mind
When rivers are not real
Requires no brilliant intellect
Nor calls for special skill.
And crossing rivers in your mind
When rivers are not there,
Makes thoughts play tricks on you, and you'll
See rivers everywhere.
Don't cross your rivers 'til you come
To where your rivers are,
But when they're real, don't fear to cross;
That's what a river's for!
And you will cross each river if
Upon some rocky ridge,
Hope sinks a shaft beside the gorge
And Faith suspends a bridge.

Open the gates, that the righteous nation which
keeps faith may enter in.　　　　**Isaiah 26:2**

Power in Prayer

The serene silent beauty of a holy life is the most powerful influence in the world next to the might of the Spirit of God. **Charles Spurgeon**

Don't pray for tasks equal to your strength but strength equal to your tasks.

WHEN CHILDREN PRAY

When little children kneel to pray
I think God is not far away.
And softest prayers their lips intone,
I think reach up to heaven's throne.
And blest are parents day by day
Who teach their children how to pray.
For children's prayers are always heard
When offered up in children's words.
And every little child that prays
Redeems the earth in countless ways,
For children, kneeling, lisping prayers
Are of all gifts our nation shares,
The surest hope, the promise grand
That God will bless and spare this land.

UNANSWERED PRAYER

Thank God for prayers He did not grant
The way I thought He should,
For I have lived to see some things
I sought weren't for my good.
Thank God for prayers which He refused,
For had He granted them
I may have treasured gifts bestowed
And turned my gaze from Him.
Thank God for answers He withheld—
The Saviour's name I bless
For prayers unanswered paved my path
To higher happiness.

ALL PRAYER IS ANSWERED

Why doubt that God answers prayer?
To most of us who pray,
He replies with a simple "No,"
Or else says, "Not today."
We complain, "But that's no answer,"
Because we're unaware
God's No or Wait is often
A perfect answer to prayer.
At other times we're burdened down
So much we pray and fast,
And God replies, "Go work it out;
You bring it to pass."
Let us give thanks for positive answers
But think it not unusual
That God's best answer often is
Postponement and refusal.

Nothing lies outside the reach of prayer except that which lies outside the will of God.

Most people commit the same mistake with God that they do with their friends—they do all the talking.
—Fulton J. Sheen

The prayer of a righteous man has great power in its effects. **James 5:16**

Proud Parenthood

There is no man, no woman, so small but that
they can make their life great by high endeavor.
Carlyle

A THOUSAND MILES AWAY

My boys would burst into my room
And find me in my chair,
And they would ask advice or tell
One of their exploits rare.
But I would wave them on and say,
Whenever they inquired,
"Perhaps you ought to run along;
Tonight I'm very tired."
And I'd go right on reading news
As they would beg to stay,
But I ignored them like they were
A thousand miles away.
Ah! things are different now and I
Would give my all in fact
To have them burst into my room
And see them trooping back.
Alas it's not to be because
My sons grew strong and tall
And moved a thousand miles away—
So far they seldom call.
And it's not that I want them here
If they are called elsewhere,
Nor is it that I doubt their love.
I'm sure they really care.
But I can't help but wonder what
The outcome might have been
If I had laid the paper down
And talked to them back then.
Of course, I can't take these things back
But for my sons I pray
That they'll each take time with their boys
Before they move away.

I GIVE MYSELF

Dear God, since you've bestowed
This tiny child on me
I seek to dedicate
This cherished gift to Thee.
And so with soul and mind
My child to Thee I bring,
But can words consecrate
So pure and dear a thing?
Yet still I offer him
In faith You'll give him grace
To early find in life
And in Thy Church a place.
But he's already Thine
And it occurs to me
It's I, dear Lord, who need
To give myself to Thee.

LET'S MAKE MARRIAGE WORK

None has a right to seek
His own self-centered joy
If he forfeits the peace
Of his own girl or boy.
But oft a child is forced
To pay the fearful price
Of his own parent's search
For new loves that entice.
Then let's make marriage work
And put our children first
And share parental love
Lest one small child be crushed.

Children, obey your parents in the Lord, for this
is right.　　　　　　　　**Ephesians 6:1**

Purpose and Principles

Only those who have the patience to do simple things perfectly, ever acquire the skills to do the difficult things easily. **Schiller**

It takes less time to do a thing right than it does to explain why you did it wrong.

Life bores only when it has no purpose.

MONUMENT BUILDING

Harsh critics threw stones at me
And I resented it,
But knew with my best efforts
That I could not prevent it.
Insight was suddenly given
That I should, with rocks flung,
Make of them stepping stones,
Or guideposts for the young.
And so I took stones tossed
At me in angry blindness,
And piled them high and built
A monument to kindness.

I SEEK NOT HAPPINESS

Some pray for happiness.
I've never prayed for that;
Instead I beg for valor,
Brave courage in combat.
For life, I've found, is war
And that's why some deserting
Run away like cowards;
The odds are disconcerting.
I seek not happiness
Though I'll admit I crave
Those stabs of joy that come
In life from being brave.

TEN YEARS IN ONE

I think I'll have to have
A thousand years or more
To reach the goals desired
Which life has set before.
And yet a hundred years
So seldom comes to men
That I must fill with work
Each year as full as ten.
Since life so brief meets not
A tenth of all my needs,
I'll cram in every year
Ten years of golden deeds.

STICKABILITY

High purpose and great goals
Are needed to succeed;
But goals are not enough,
There is another need.
Initiative and drive
Or plain "get up and go"
Are also factors of
Success, as most men know.
Still there's another gift
To win the victor's cup;
It's stickability
And never giving up.

It is almost as presumptuous to think you can do nothing as to think you can do everything.

—Phillips Brooks

It is easier to fight for one's principles than to live up to them. —Alfred Adler

The Lord will fulfil his purpose for me. **Psalms 138:8**

Quest for Quality

The chains of habit are generally too small to be felt until they are too strong to be broken.

Samuel Johnson

HIS LEVEL BEST

He never said a lot
Nor sought to be well known,
But when he had a job
He could be counted on.
He never tried to lead
Or boast that he was smart,
But everything he did
He did with all his heart.
He never sought men's praise
Like many of the rest,
But in all things he did,
He did his level best.

No man is worth his salt who is not ready at all times to risk his body, to risk his well-being, to risk his life in a great cause.

—Theodore Roosevelt

BE NEGATIVE

Learn to say No! the world's in need
Of men who know a good from evil deed.
Learn to say No! And then stick to it,
Unmoved when men say, "Everybody's doing it."
Learn to say No! and don't delay it;
Fence-straddling fails; then stand and say it;
Learn to say No! nor fear derision;
Stick bravely with your bold decision.
Learn to say No! We've waited long
For souls God-fearing, who hate the wrong.
Learn to say No! and in double measure
Christ's joy will be your constant treasure.

GROW TALL! AIM HIGH! BE TRUE!

Grow tall, young man, grow tall!
We're all beholding you
And God's upholding you
That you need never fall.
Aim high, young man, aim high!
For we take pride in you
That truth abides in you
Which you exemplify.
Be true, young man, be true!
For our sick world in need
Now looks to you, indeed,
To go and make it new.

DO YOUR BEST

What can a person do?
He can't do very much
But if he'll do his best
Then that is good enough.
What can one person do?
He can't do every task
But if he'll do his best
That's all the Lord will ask.
What can one person do?
Each one can do his best
And he'll find life is good
And with God be the rest.

Happiness is a butterfly, which, when pursued, is always just beyond your grasp, but which, if you will sit down quietly, may alight upon you.

—Hawthorne

He who trusts in the Lord will be enriched.

Proverbs 28:25

Quit Quarreling

People generally quarrel because they cannot argue.   **G. K. Chesterton**

If good people learned to be agreeable it would win many to the good cause.

The worst-tempered people I've ever met were people who knew they were wrong.

—Wilson Mizner

TWO KINDS OF PEOPLE

The housefly is a pest
And is despised as such,
For it blights everything
Its legs and wings may touch.
But bees still pollinate
On cloudy days and sunny
The clover and the corn
And manufacture honey.
We're all like busy bees
Or else like unclean flies.
Are you a honey-maker
Or spreading filth and lies?

SATAN'S FAITH

The faith that lets us sin
Against a brother weak
Can hardly be the faith
Of Christ the lowly Meek.
The faith that makes some glad
To see a brother fall
Can hardly be the faith
Of Christ who brothered all.
The faith that makes some seek
To harm a fellow man
Is more like Satan's faith—
But far from Christ's command.

ENVIRONMENT

Grouch was the family name;
Grim was the oldest brother,
And Greed and Gripe were twins;
Grump was their name for mother.
Beside them lived the Spats
Whose sons were Spit and Spite;
The girls were Sass and Stew
And how they loved to fight.
They lived in Peevish town
(To live there I would waiver)
For Grouches hate the Spats
And Spats return the favor.

To interfere with the quarrels of relatives is to go through life without a friend.

You can't prove anything in an argument except that you're just as bullheaded as the other fellow.

WHERE I FOUND GOD

With scorn I built a wall
Excluding undesirables,
And I, shut-in with God,
Reread all of my Bibles.
I had misgivings though
And so, one day in doubt
I climbed my wall to see
Vile things I had shut out.
'Twas there amidst outcasts
I saw the Lord of All—
The God I thought I had
Confined behind my wall.

Why are you troubled, and why do questionings arise in your hearts?   **Luke 24:38**

Quitters Questioned

Now, God be thanked, who has matched us with His hour!   **Rupert Brooke**

THE COURAGE NOT TO FLEE

I'd rather be a slave
Shackled by my slavery,
Than flee my post of duty
When life demanded bravery.
I'd rather venture not
Than withdraw half-discouraged
From life's great battlefield,
Convinced I lacked true courage.
I'd sooner die ten deaths
At hands of foes empowered,
Rather than live for years
Convinced I was a coward.

Anyone can carry his burden, however hard, until nightfall. Anyone can live sweetly, patiently, lovingly, purely till the sun goes down. And this is all that life really means.
                                        —Robert Louis Stevenson

THE CLIMBERS

It's strange how victories won
Can tempt us more or less
To quit and rest content
With our new-found success.
Complacency sets in
When we some goal have gained,
Though it should make us seek
High goals yet unattained.
Then let's not rest on laurels
But seek new heights sublime,
For all were made to strive
And never cease to climb.

There are three types of people: those who make things happen, those who watch things happen, and the vast majority, who have no idea what happens.

THOUGH OTHERS QUIT

Don't be a quitter! The world awaits
A man with steadfast will
Who still pursues the shining goal
When quitters leave the field.
Don't be a quitter! You must be brave
When guns begin to rattle;
For just when men are needed most
The quitters flee the battle.
Stand up and fight though others quit
And timid souls grow bitter;
Stand at your post though you are slain,
But don't become a quitter.

DON'T CRY, DON'T FEAR, DON'T QUIT

When trouble seems to double,
And trouble is contagious,
There's something we can do
And that is be courageous.
Of course, some rain must fall
But we can be greathearted,
And help the quitters start
Who need to get restarted.
When trouble seems to double
And you see you can't win,
Don't cry, don't fear, don't quit.
Take courage and try again.

They who wait for the Lord shall renew their strength, they shall mount up with wings like eagles, they shall run and not be weary, they shall walk and not faint.   **Isaiah 40:31**

Redemption Realized

Death is not a journeying into an unknown land; it is a voyage home. We are going not to a strange country, but to our Father's house, and among our kith and kin.   **John Ruskin**

I have always thought that faith in immortality is proof of the sanity of a man's nature.
                                        —Emerson

WE'LL KNOW THEM

When life's short day is done
And it's our time to go
We'll cross the threshold o'er
And not one fear we'll know.
For just inside the door
Friends we have lost a while
Will greet and welcome us,
A parent, friend, or child.
And though some mock this faith
Yet we without one fear
Are sure we'll know them all
And hold them very near.

WHAT DEATH IS LIKE

I asked what death is like
And saw the eveningtide
Stoop down caressing earth
All sad and lone and tired.
I asked what death is like
And saw a fresh sunrise
That came expelling night
And waking sleeping eyes.
I asked what death is like
And saw a shadowed face
Of One I recognized,
A friend I should embrace.

My gems are falling away; but it is because God is making up His jewels.   —Charles Wolfe

WHERE DEATHLESS LIFE BEGINS

Death is not death to those who trust,
It's just an open door,
A gateway to the place God dwells
With loved ones gone before.
Death is not death to those who have
A faith, expelling fears;
It's finding sleep that soon awakes
Where God erases tears.
Death is not death to souls who trust;
To them it's just a ride,
A pleasant trip to mansions fair
Where loved ones wait inside.
And death's not death to those who die
In love with Christ their Friend;
To them it's just the starting point
Where deathless life begins.

There is a land where everlasting suns shed everlasting brightness; where the soul drinks from the living streams of love that roll by God's high throne!—myriads of glorious ones bring their accepted offering. Oh! how blest to look from this dark prison to that shrine, to inhale one breath of Paradise divine, and enter into that eternal rest which waits the sons of God!
                                        —John Bowring

For with the Lord there is steadfast love, and with him is plenteous redemption.
                                        Psalms 130:7

Reflections on Retirement

There is one art of which every man should be a master—the art of reflection.

Samuel Taylor Coleridge

OLD ENOUGH TO BEGIN

At ten we're much too old
For blocks and baby toys;
At twenty we're too old
For pleasures kids enjoy.
At thirty we're too old
To run a track-meet mile,
And most at forty seem
For football out of style.
By fifty we're too old
For toughest tennis game,
And most at sixty are
For basketball the same.
But sixty is the age
That some to college start,
And some at seventy begin
To hike and master art.
Some at eighty research
Until they write a book;
Some ninety, paint and fish,
Or garden by a brook.
Each age of life fulfills
Unfolding, human needs,
And each new stage of life
Prepares for nobler deeds.

Cherish all your happy moments. They will make a fine cushion for old age.

—Booth Tarkington

Those who enjoy the large pleasures of advanced age are those who have sacrificed the small pleasures of youth.   —Charles E. Carpenter

HE'LL MAKE TOMORROW GOOD

Why should I be afraid
Of what the future holds,
For through these years I've found
God's will each day unfolds.
And as I've lived today
With faith that conquers fears
So I will face tomorrow
And future untried years.
I'll fearless face the future
Persuaded and assured
That God of yesteryears
Will make tomorrow good.

I DO NOT WALK ALONE

Because God walked with me
Through all my yesteryears,
I now look back and read
The meaning of my tears.
Because God walks with me
Within this present day,
I face these tough times, sure
He guides me in this way.
Because God walks with me
Into some paths unknown,
They hold no fear for me;
I do not walk alone.

And your old men shall dream dreams.

Acts 2:17

Religious Reality

Calvary shows how far men will go in sin, and how far God will go for man's salvation.

Henry Clay Trumbull

WE NEED ACQUAINTANCESHIP

Does faith mean mouthing creeds
Because they're very old,
Or quoting ancient scripture
Inscribed on ancient scrolls?
Does faith mean facts believed
Which history can't confirm,
Or gulping dogmas down
Which conscience can't affirm?
But surely faith is more
Than trust in facts of history,
Or giving mental nods
To miracles clothed with mystery.
We need the Christian Scriptures
And none should call them odd,
But we need Christian experience,
A first-hand knowledge of God.
We need acquaintanceship
With God in such a way
That knowledge of Him is
More than merely hearsay.
Such faith for most of us,
Alas, is too high priced.
Quoting creeds is much easier
Than following Christ.

God is more interested in making us what He wants us to be than giving us what we ought to have. —Walter Wilson

I DRIVE THIS TRUCK FOR HIM

"What do you do for Christ each day?"
A fervent Christian said,
And I replied, "I drive a truck
And fill the stores with bread."
"I know," he said, "of your bread route,
But that is not the thing;
I mean what do you do each day
For Jesus Christ the King?"
I said, "But I believe a man
Can work in such a way
That selling bread is Christian work,
A sacrament each day."
Again the man inquired, "But, Sir,
If this is not unfair,
What do you do for Christ each day,
Like witnessing and prayer?"
"Work is my witness plain," I said,
"And selling bread to them
Is like a prayer in Jesus' name;
I drive this truck for Him."

God's ultimate purpose is unchanging but his strategy may vary infinitely.

—Peter Taylor Forsyth

And the peace of God, which passes all understanding, will keep your hearts and your minds in Christ Jesus. **Philippians 4:7**

ut of all the gifts to you, you shall present every offering due to the Lord. **Numbers 18:29**

SMALL GIFTS ARE BEST

I'd like to give away
As long as I should live
Great gifts of wealth and land,
But it's not mine to give.
Yet every day I will
From my most meager store
Give gifts of love in faith
That God will give me more.
And how I pity those
Who seek large gifts to spare
And miss the larger joy
Of giving their small share.

Make your vows to the Lord your God, and perform them: let all around him bring gifts.
Psalms 76:11

Rest and Reunion

There are no crown-wearers in heaven that were
not cross-bearers here below. **Charles Spurgeon**

There is only one way to get ready for immortality, and that is to love this life and live it as bravely and faithfully and cheerfully as we can.

—van Dyke

RESTLESSNESS

God grants a restlessness to birds
To flee the winterlands,
And guides them through the pathless sky
And guards them with His hands.
God grants a restlessness to birds
To venture into space,
And when He calls the birds down South
He fixes them a place.
God grants a restlessness to men
To fly across life's sea
And some arise assured they'll find
Their home, dear Lord, in Thee.
And we may each on wings of faith
In hopes of life beyond
Obey the restless urge we feel
And to God's call respond.
For we, like migrant flocks of birds,
Are called to flee from strife;
Birds find a South prepared for them.
Men find eternal life.

We are born for a higher destiny than of earth. There is a realm where the rainbow never fades, where the stars will be spread before us like islands that slumber on the ocean, and where the beings that now pass over before us like shadows will stay in our presence forever.

—Edward George Bulwer-Lytton

HE TALKED OF LIFE

Christ mostly talked of life;
That's what the people needed,
And what He taught rang true;
That's why so many heeded.
And He exemplified
His words with each kind deed
'Til men beheld His life
And then embraced His creed.
He talked so much of life
And such assurance gave
That sinners trusting Him
Went fearless to their grave.

The veil which conceals the future from us is woven by the hands of mercy.

I THINK I'LL GO ALONG

When death presents its card
Announcing its intention
I think I'll go along
Without one fear to mention.
But if I have my share
Of ordinary fears
They'll be from facing paths
Untrod through unlived years.
Yet I trust God and pray
When death states its intention,
I'll just unlatch the door
Without one apprehension.

The Lord your God is providing you a place of
rest. **Joshua 1:13**

Resurrection Revealed

Our Lord has written the promise of the resurrection, nor in books alone, but in every leaf in springtime.   **Martin Luther**

Jesus lives! Henceforth is death but the gate of life immortal.   —Gellert

ASSURANCE

I know He lives but how I know
May seem a strange surprise;
I've seen His Easter glory shine
In happy children's eyes.
I know He lives but how I know
To some means not a thing;
Yet proof conclusive comes
Each time I witness Spring.
I know He lives but how I know
May not each critic please;
All nature sings the Easter song,
'Tis swelled on every breeze.
But best of all I know He lives
For in this heart of mine
He rose with healing in His wings
And I, Lord Christ, am Thine.

HE ROSE IN MAJESTY

He rose in majesty
To live forevermore
And He turned prison walls
Into an open door.
Salvation's door swings wide
And those who enter find
His cross is love's best proof,
The empty tomb its sign.
He rose in majesty
And now upon His throne
He draws us with His love
And claims us for His own.

IT ALL BEGAN WITH CHRIST

All history's hinges turn
On doors of that rude stall;
All streams of justice flow
From Pilate's judgement hall.
All freedom has its roots
Deep in the Holy Land;
All strength to uplift men
Depends on nail-pierced hands.
Life's purpose, worth, and joy
First dawned that Easter morn,
And every cross makes sense
Since Christ was crowned with thorns.

HE MADE A HIGHWAY

Christ made a cross of shame
Into a royal throne
And from that cross as King
He claims us for His own.
Christ took a twisted fate
And as the Son of man
Suspended in the sky
He drew salvation's plan.
Christ took the dead-end street
That ended in death's gloom
And carved a thoroughfare wide
Into the Father's room.

It is a great thing to know that if the eternal doors swing wide open the other way for you, you have a Friend on the other side waiting to receive you.   —Howard Kelly

You will be repaid at the resurrection of the just.   **Luke 14:14**

Romance of Righteousness

Many persons have a wrong idea about what constitutes true happiness. It is not attained through self-gratification, but through fidelity to a worthy purpose. **Helen Keller**

TO WITNESS WITH LIFE

You never mentioned faith
And yet I say sincerely,
I have stronger faith.
Your life has witnessed clearly.
You never mentioned kindness
And yet in some strange fashion
You've witnessed with your life
Of Christ and His compassion.
You never mentioned Jesus,
Yet I in spiritual blindness
Have found my sight restored,
And Christ revealed through kindness.

To walk the straight and narrow path is far better than to move in the best circles.

TRUSTING GOD

God calls us not to peace alone
Where joys abide with pains unknown.
God bids us not to dwell always
Where bluebirds sing through sunshine days.
But God calls us to live these years
Trusting Him in spite of fears.
We're called to live a life of trust
Believing God provides for us.

What we have done for ourselves alone dies with us; what we have done for others and the world remains and is immortal.   —Albert Pike

Living is doing even while we say there is nothing we can do; we stumble over the opportunities for service that we are passing by in our tear-blinded self-pity.   —Ray Winningham

I CAUGHT YOUR FAITH

I saw you stand steadfast in grief
But saw no trace of unbelief.
I saw you stand unmoved by stress
But saw no trace of bitterness.
I saw you stand bravely for years
But saw no trace of senseless fears.
Though you spoke not of faith's firm law,
I caught your faith by things I saw.

NOT "WHY" BUT "HOW"

I've left the land of "Why"
And now affirm this vow,
I go to dwell by faith
Within the land of "How."
Too long I've cried, "Why, God,
Did you do this to me?"
Henceforth I'll pray, "How, God,
May I use this for Thee?"
What happens doesn't count
And "Why" is not the test;
It's "How" I take each thing
That makes me cursed or blest.

We lose the peace of years when we hunt after the rapture of moments.   —Bulwer-Lytton

Be not rash with your mouth, nor let your heart be hasty to utter a word before God, for God is in heaven, and you upon the earth; therefore let your words be few. **Ecclesiastes 5:2**

Saviour and Sinners

While salvation is free, it is not cheap.

I FOUND ABUNDANT LIFE

With plans devised and courage bold,
I ventured forth to gain my goal,
Of earning wealth and winning fame
And bringing glory to my name,
Until one day I met the Christ
And found in Him abundant life.
With schemes and plans that left out God,
I lived for self nor thought it odd
That I, without a thought of halting,
Felt justified in self-exalting,
Until one day I met the Christ
And found in Him abundant life.
I did not care what price I paid
To have my will and way always,
Nor did I question any scheme
If it fulfilled my selfish dream,
Until one day I met the Christ
And found in Him abundant life.
He broke my stubborn will completely
When in my heart He whispered sweetly,
"Behold My dying on the cross
For you that you may not be lost."
It was that instant I trusted Christ
And found in Him abundant life.

It's easier to sail the Atlantic in a paper boat
than to get to heaven on good works.

I GAVE MYSELF

Wise men of old followed the gleam
Gambling their life upon a dream,
That if by faith they ventured far
Their God would guide them with a star
Unto the place of sacrifice
Where they could offer gifts to Christ.
I've seen no star in Christmas skies;
My faith is but a weak surmise;
Nor have I glimpsed some special sign;
No dazzling stars for me e'er shine.
Yet, I by faith in some strange sense
Have offered gold and frankincense,
Or else like one with alabaster
I gave myself and found my Master.

I STOOD UP FOR HIS NAME

Some heard a mystic voice
Or felt God's hand divine,
While others dreamed a dream
Or glimpsed some holy sign.
But not one thing I saw
Except myself condemned,
A sinner without hope,
Sincerely needing Him.
'Twas then I, who had been
Of Jesus Christ ashamed,
Renounced my sin and pride
And stood up for His name.

*Bless the Lord, O my soul; and all that is within
me, bless his holy name!*   **Psalms 103:1**

Secrets of Sharing

I have tried to keep things in my hands and lost them all, but what I have given into God's hands I still possess.　　**Martin Luther**

PUT UP OR SHUT UP

When I said, "I feel bad
For the plight of the poor,"
One said, "Your feeling bad
Is admirable for sure.
But if you feel for them
As you so sadly look,
Perhaps you ought to feel
Inside your pocket book."
It was then I saw myself
With talk as cheap as trash;
I'd felt bad for the poor
But never felt for cash.

TO UNDERSTAND IS TO SHARE

He came with great perplexity
And whispered, "I'm discouraged;
In fact, I'm quitting completely
Unless I find fresh courage."
But what could I offer him?
I offered silent prayer
That I'd know how to help him
Who faced desperate despair.
Finally, I whispered through tears,
"But I and every man
Have faced a similar situation.
I think I understand."
Surprised, he smiled, "Thanks a lot!
You've given me great encouragement.
I thought I was all alone.
You've shared my discouragement."

The first lesson in Christ's school is self-denial.
　　　　　—Matthew Henry

WHERE I SAW GOD

Today I saw a man
Freezing in a storm,
And I gave him my coat
And made him very warm.
Today I saw a child
Begging on a street,
And I gave him a coin
That he might buy and eat.
I saw my God today
But not in usual form;
I saw Him in a child
And met Him in a storm.

You give but little when you give of your possessions. It is when you give of yourself that you truly give.
　　　　　—Kahil Gibran

WING-BORNE AND HEALED

So you're downcast with grief
Though you try not to be?
You say you can't face life?
Then please pay heed to me.
In grief, I found one grieving,
A friend whom I resolved
To comfort, help, and strengthen,
And lo, my grief was solved.
Then go and comfort others,
Some friend bowed down with sorrow,
And you'll find your bruised heart
Wing-borne and healed tomorrow.

Live in harmony with one another; do not be haughty, but associate with the lowly.　　**Romans 12:16**

Sentimental Sighs

*How can such deep-imprinted images sleep in us
at times, till a word, a sound, awake them?*
Gotthold E. Lessing

MY HEART HAS BLED

Whatever friends may say of me,
Whate'er my foes have said,
They haven't told enough until
They say my heart has bled.
It seems my heart has bled enough
To make the rivers flow;
Yet from each drop that stains my path
White lilies seem to grow.
And shattered dreams that came to me,
Which bruised and crushed my heart,
Have seemed like messengers from God
With wisdom to impart.
I think it's when hearts bleed, Christ calls,
"Come share My easy yoke;"
And it is then we let Him heal
The heart that sorrow broke.
It's then we cry, "The kingdom's Thine
Who heals our hearts that ache;
It's doubly Thine, for Your brave heart
Once on a cross did break."

Memory is a capricious and arbitrary creature.
You never can tell what pebble she will pick up
from the shore of life to keep among her trea-
sures, or what inconspicuous flower of the field
she will preserve as the symbol of "thoughts that
do often lie too deep for tears." . . . And yet I
do not doubt that the most important things are
always the best remembered.

—Henry Van Dyke

HIDE-AND-SEEK

Of childhood joys I cherish,
I often think and speak
Of rainy days and cold
When we played hide-and-seek.
What fun we had back then
With playmates that we loved,
Hiding 'neath beds and tables,
And in the attic above.
Nostalgic rainy days
Remind of friendly faces,
When we played hide-and-seek
And hid in funny places.

THE OLD HEARTHSTONE

From childhood's vanished years
On memory's golden wings
There floats to my mind's eye
Some cherished childhood scenes.
The scene I love the best
While musing all alone
Is of my family dear
Circling the old hearthstone.
Back then when day was done,
Around that old fireplace
We'd sit and talk while flames
Cast shadows on our face.
Fireplaces meant so much;
Our country needs them now
With families joining hands
Around hearthstones of prayer.

*Lord, all my longing is known to thee, my sighing
is not hidden from thee.* **Psalms 38:9**

Sights and Scenes

In all the ranks of life the human heart yearns for the beautiful; and the beautiful things that God makes are his gift to all alike.

Harriet Beecher Stowe

OLD TIME FRIENDS

I love to think of things
As they were long ago,
Mantel clocks that chimed,
Fire-places all aglow.
Cane-bottom chairs, hand-made,
And lamps fresh-trimmed and lit,
Soft prayers at supper time,
Fire-wood, chopped-up and split.
Familiar childhood paths,
A pond in which we swam,
Smokehouses seeping smoke,
Hung with some well-smoked hams.
Children lisping prayers,
White sheets on sagging beds,
Fragrant breakfast odors,
Preserves on home-made bread.
I love to think of things,
Old-timey things back then,
But best of all I love
To think of old-time friends.

Home is the place where each should live for all and all should live for God.

Home is the place where we grumble the most and are loved the most.

The thrill of getting back home is by far the most enjoyable feature of a summer vacation.

I'VE HAD MY FILL

Of city life I've had enough,
It's back to the country for me,
Where I can breathe deep as I can
Of air that's fresh and free.
Of business rush I've had enough
And traffic-laden streets,
Where honking horns and engine fumes
And worn-out tempers meet.
Then give me back the country splendor
Fenced with the sentinel hills,
Where sun-splashed trees shade quiet woods
That border fresh-plowed fields.
Of city life I've had enough
With tension, greed and strife;
Lord, free me from this man-made hell.
Give me the country life.

THE HEART OF AMERICA

I sought the heart of this great land
But found it not where I had planned.
On rich Wall Street I walked apart
Sure that was not my nation's heart.
In Washington, sweet freedom's shrine,
My country's heart I failed to find.
At last my nation's heart I found
In homes where love and prayers abound.

He has made everything beautiful in its time.
Ecclesiastes 3:11

Spreading Salvation

It is a great deal better to live a holy life than to talk about it. Lighthouses do not ring bells and fire cannon to call attention to their shining— they just shine.   **Dwight L. Moody**

CHRIST BELONGS ON THE STREET

A famous sculptor carved in stone
A statue of the Christ,
A masterpiece soon purchased by
A church at costly price.
Those churchmen thought that if they owned
A work of art so rare
Huge crowds would throng their church to see
The gleaming statue there.
But very few came to admire
The Christ fashioned from stone,
So on the altar stood the Lord
In splendor, all alone.
That year a fire burned out the church
And members all assumed,
That all was lost until they found
The statue unconsumed.
Out on the 'lawn beside the street
They brought the masterpiece
And all who passed beheld the Christ,
A throng that never ceased.
Some went away with hopes restored,
Some found their Lord that day,
And some brought friends that they may see
And some went home to pray.
A churchman wept, "We've long concealed
The Christ upon the altar,
Concealed the Lord by stained glass art
But now we will not falter
To leave Him here out on the street,
For He's the whole world's friend,
And may we let stained glass no more
Obscure the Christ again."

THE CHURCH WITHOUT A ROOF

In World War II at Anzio
Three soldiers wounded there
Limped to a bombed cathedral
For worship and for prayer.
The Jew was blind; the Catholic lost
Both hands in war's commotion;
The Protestant was crippled bad
Due to a bomb explosion.
The blinded Jew supported him
Whose legs were crushed and drawn,
And he whose handless arms were bound
Led him whose sight was gone.
Without his arms the Catholic boy
God's Presence could not find,
That is until the blinded Jew
Fashioned the cross's sign.
The sightless Jew would hear the law
But who would read his scroll?
So he with legs crushed volunteered
And fed a Jewish soul.
No preacher came to share God's bread
Around the holy table,
Yet still the Protestant would go
But sensed he was not able.
But that brave youth inched down the aisle
Helped by a Jewish hand,
And guiding him were Catholic eyes
Who showed them where to stand.
None cared what name that burned church bore
Whose only roof was sky;
That day their needs exceeded creeds
And each found God was nigh.

As your faith increases, our field among you may be greatly enlarged, so that we may preach the gospel in lands beyond you.   **2 Corinthians 10:15–16**

Strength of Solitude

A quiet spirit is of inestimable value in carrying on outward activities.　Hannah Whitall Smith

I have often regretted my speech, never my silence. 　　　　—Publilius Syrus

If you must talk about your troubles, don't bore your friends with them. They aren't impressed. Tell your enemies. They'll be delighted.

HEART'S DESIRE

I've craved no house beside the road,
I'm sure I never will;
I seek a quiet sequestered spot—
A house high on a hill.
I long to get away from things
And on some hilltop tarry,
Until I feel God's presence near,
And darkness floods the valley.
Then grant me such a house and let
Me go apart and stand
In presence of unhurried things,
Far from the cries of man,
And I'll arise each morn refreshed,
At peace with man and God,
And turn my steps back to the city
Where sad men, friendless, plod.
I'll stand where troubled souls rush by
And be a friend to them,
If God should grant my heart's desire—
A hilltop house with Him.

THE CHRISTIAN GLOW

The darkest night cannot put out
One tiny candle light;
Dark nights enhance a candle flame
And make the flicker bright.
So this dark world of sin cannot
Put out a Christian's glow;
My soul's dark night just helped me shine
And let God's Kingdom grow.

SECRETS OF SOLITUDE

Instead of loneliness
When lonely years are viewed,
Great souls term aloneness
As a blest solitude.
Such ones are seldom lonely
And drink so deep of gladness
That aloneness is for them
An exemption from sadness.
And they look back remembering
The thrill of being alone,
And call it solitude
When lonely days have flown.
Secrets of solitude
Dear Lord I'd learn from Thee,
Who fasted for forty days
And braved Gethsemane.

OH WHAT A FOOL WAS I!

Releasing butterflies
I've torn cocoons apart
But larvae always died
I tried to give a start.
I helped a bud unfold,
But noticed by and by
My fingers left a blight
That made the bud to die.
A friend who sought my love
I gave advice instead;
Oh what a fool was I!
For now our friendship's dead.

In quietness and in trust shall be your strength.
Isaiah 30:15

Tender Thoughts

Marriage resembles a pair of shears, so joined that they can not be separated; often moving in opposite directions, yet always punishing anyone who comes between them. **Sydney Smith**

TO MOTHER ON MOTHER'S DAY

The thoughtfulness you've shown
Grows sweeter everyday,
Until my debt of love
Has grown too large to pay.
I owe a debt to you
For every thoughtful prayer
And deeds you've done for me
Expressing tender care.
And though I cannot pay,
Yet love must be expressed;
You are to me this day
The dearest and the best.

UNLESS THE HEART IS KIND

Your kindness is far more
Than words which reach the mind;
Words are so meaningless
Unless the heart is kind.
'Til one is kind to you
When you are in distress
You'll never know just how
Your words of kindness bless.
Your unremembered words
Are treasured by me yet,
And kind deeds that you do
I never shall forget.

A successful marriage requires falling in love many times, always with the same person.
—Mignon McLaughlin

Keep thy eyes wide open before marriage, and half shut afterwards. —Benjamin Franklin

SILENCE NURTURES LOVE

It's not just words you say
Which tell me how you feel,
Your silence speaks volumes,
Deep truths words can't reveal.
Great love like music great,
Requires pauses of silence;
So silence nurtures love
As harsh speech nurtures violence.
Quiet-like, our hearts commune
And by your loving gaze
Convincingly you speak
To me in silent ways.

YOU'RE THE GREATEST

We celebrate birthdays
Of those we say are great,
Yet yours is not observed
By nation or by state.
But what are halls of fame
In light of love you share?
You live in hearts of friends.
Love has enshrined you there.
"Who's Who" you have not earned
And wealth you may not get,
Yet I on your birthday
Think you're the greatest yet.

Love does not insist on its own way.
1 Corinthians 13:5

Tested and Tried

There is not one life which the Life-giver ever loses out of His sight: not one which sins so that He casts it away; not one which is not so near to Him that whatever touches it touches Him with sorrow or with joy. **Phillips Brooks**

BEHOLDING THE LIKENESS

In ancient times when ore was crushed
With firm and fearful blow
They'd place it in a crucible
And make the furnace glow.
They heated it until the gold
Was melted from the dross,
And skilled refiners skimmed away
The worthless molten loss.
In fact he'd skim and skim until
No dross was left and he
Could look upon the liquid gold
And there his countenance see.
So Christ the great refiner of
The sinful human heart
Skims all the dross of sin away
And purges every part.
Sometimes I cry, "Lord Christ, how long
Must I this flame endure?"
And He replies with tear-dimmed eyes,
"Until your heart is pure."
But why this way?" I've often asked
When I've borne all I could;
He says, "But it's the Father's will
And it is for your good."
God help me stand these trials if soon
My Saviour may behold
His love reflected in my face,
His image on my soul.

To bear pain without letting it spoil your happiness is true valor.

It is not the will of God to give us more troubles than will bring us to live by faith in Him; He loves us too well to give us a moment of uneasiness for our good.
—Jules Romains

ALL WILL BE CLEAR

Ask not the question "Why?"
For someday up above
We'll see the reason why
And say that God is love.
Ask not the question "Why?"
For after life's brief spell
We'll be with God and know
That He does all things well.
Ask not the question "Why?"
But trust God like a child,
And all will be made clear
In just a little while.

THE QUESTION

A path on which men walked each day
Said to a rose crushed by the way,
"You smell so sweet! How can it be?"
The rose replied, "Men walk on me."
"They walk on me," the sad path wept,
"But it makes me harder each step."
I pondered this until I asked,
"Am I the rose or like the path?"

But he knows the way that I take; when he has tried me, I shall come forth as gold. **Job 23:10**

nd when they lifted up their eyes, they saw no one but Jesus only. **Matthew 17:8**

TO LOVE HIM LIKE JOHN

As Matthew, Mark, Luke and John
Wrote words exalting Christ,
So we as Christians daily draw
Our portrait of His life.
With words they spread His faith afar
For they were very gifted;
We now with deeds of eloquence
Must see that He's uplifted.
But that we may exalt His name
Which Christians all profess,
We must if we would win the world
Pass a simple test.
Do we like Matthew live for Him?
Or win souls like Mark won?
Or will we follow Him like Luke?
Or love Him like Saint John?

Truly, I say to you, among those born of woman there has risen no one greater than John the Baptist; yet he who is least in the kingdom of heaven is greater than he. **Matthew 11:11**

Thrill of Teaching

The art of teaching is not imparting truth but imparting a thirst for truth.

The object of teaching a child is to enable him to get along without a teacher.

—Elbert Hubbard

BUCKLE DOWN

So you are called to teach,
But are you qualified?
First, are you teachable?
Is that not still required?
Do you with all your heart
And with all your speech
Exemplify each day
The doctrines that you teach?
But let's take one step more;
Can you pass this tough test?
Are you dissatisfied
When you have done your best?
And will you if you teach
Give all your talent to it?
If you can answer, "Yes,"
You're called; buckle down! do it.

The best and most important part of every man's education is that which he gives himself.

—Edward Gibbon

Education is something you get when your father sends you to college but it isn't complete until you send your son there.

SAY SOMETHING POSITIVE

Have you a positive word?
Then let me quickly hear it;
Too long negative thinking
Has depressed my spirit.
Have you a helpful word?
Then let me hear you speak;
Too many cutting words
Have left me sad and weak.
Have you a song of hope?
Then let me hear you sing;
God knows today I need
To hear uplifting things.

Good teachers cost much but poor teachers cost more.

TO POISON A CHILD

What if I with some poison
Defiled my children's food?
The courts would brand me criminal—
Unfit to be excused.
Yet I with impure thoughts
Can poison my child's mind,
And go on unsuspected
Of vilest deed unkind.
Yet poisoning children's food,
Or water that he's drinking,
Is certainly no more dangerous
Than poisoning children's thinking.

Conduct yourselves wisely toward outsiders, making the most of the time. **Colossians 4:5**

Triumph Over Tragedy

*Pleasures make folk acquainted with each other,
but it takes trials and griefs to make them know
each other.*

"Josh Billings" (Henry Wheeler Shaw)

Only the soul that knows the mighty grief can
know the mighty rapture. Sorrow comes to
stretch out spaces in the heart of joy.

—Edwin Markham

A PARABLE OF LIFE

Passengers below the deck
Huddled as the ship,
Storm-tossed, made them afraid
They'd not survive the trip.
Yet one lad in their midst
Courageous, though quite small,
Climbed back on deck as if
He weren't afraid at all.
Soon he returned and smiled,
"The Captain's my Father, you see.
We need not be afraid.
The Captain just smiled at me."

A PRECIOUS CHAIR

We've heard of rocking chairs
Praised with the pen and tongue
But I sing of a chair
That usually goes unsung.
In this wheel-chair he sat,
My little boy so lame,
Nor offered one complaint
From dawn 'til evening came.
But God loved him so well
He called my child so fair,
But since he waved farewell
I've loved his small wheel-chair.

TEARS HID WITH SMILES

Today we'll meet someone
Possessed with outward calm,
Who, inwardly, is gripped
With fears and great alarm.
And we'll pass, unaware
Of woes confronting him,
Nor grasp the stinging grief
That's left his future grim.
But playing well his game,
And with his dread concealed,
We'll greet and pass not knowing
He bears deep wounds unhealed.
Today, we'll meet someone
Of whom we'll learn long after,
His tears were hid with smiles,
Grief was disguised with laughter.

DEEPER ROOTS

Tree roots grow deeper still
And take on stronger form
When trees are lashed by winds
And bruised by freezing storms.
Like trees that deeper grow
By straining in the sod,
I, too, bowed low, sank roots
Deep in the heart of God.

Life's greatest tragedy is to lose God and not
miss Him.

*Supplement your faith with virtue, and virtue
with knowledge, and knowledge with self-control.*

2 Peter 5–6

Truth About Time

The years teach much which the days never know.
Ralph Waldo Emerson

LIFE IS A STORY BOOK

Life is a story book
And with the dawning light
God gives to each of us
A clean new page to write.
Each year a chapter ends
And all we've written there
Can never be erased,
So let us write with care.
Then write great words and deeds,
Not hate or theft or bribery,
That all we write may be
Fit for heaven's great library.

PLANNING FOR THE FUTURE

While many hit the ceiling
About their low estate,
Bewailing past defeats
And cursing God and Fate,
Yet I'd be more discreet
By looking far beyond
And planning for success
That I believe will come.
I'll waste no time reflecting
On days when I was beat;
I dream of future victories,
Not yesterday's defeats.

Leisure time is no longer a problem. Thanks to modern methods of transportation, you use it all up getting to and from work.

—Fletcher Krebel

The times in which we live are decadent. It is evident we are approaching the end of the age. Everyone has disregarded the law. Children no longer obey their parents. Everyone is eager to write a book.

—Inscribed on Chaldean tablet, 2000 B.C.

DONKEY SUBLIME

Astride my back He rode to town
With garments strewn upon the ground;
Hosannas split the silent sky
And children sang with palms held high.
That ancient day I did not grasp
The greatness of my lowly task;
'Twas years and years 'til I was sure
My place in history was secure.
For as I plodded down the way
I had not sense to hope or pray
That my small task through endless time
Could make a donkey seem sublime.
Yet who can see a donkey plod
And not think of the Son of God?
And some recall that ancient day
Each time they hear a donkey bray.

SAD BUT TRUE

I think we have life's values mixed
Much like the store with price tags switched.
It seems some boys pulling a gag
Slipped in a store and switched each tag;
Next day men laughed at ten cent suits,
Ten dollar socks and nickle boots.
So life's price tags have been abused.
Values aren't real. We're all confused.

Thus says the Lord: Behold, I set before you the way of life.
Jeremiah 21:8

Unbelief and Understanding

If we could read the secret history of our enemies, we should find in each man's life sorrow and suffering enough to disarm all hostility.
Henry Wadsworth Longfellow

FAITH COMES THROUGH READING

I prayed for faith but when I finished
I found my weak faith had diminished.
I preached on faith with words dramatic
But my stale faith grew still more static.
I gave a tithe and quoted creeds
And taught a class and did good deeds
In earnest hope the faith I sought
Would crown my life through good deeds wrought.
The secret rare at last I found
That helps faith grow by leaps and bounds.
As I began to read God's Word,
Though skeptics say this seems absurd,
And as I learned to meditate
I found a weak faith growing great.
And now I know by God's great mercy
Christ comes to us through Scripture verses.
It took me years to find the key,
The Word of God brought faith to me.

CHILDREN UNDERSTAND

When faith was too complex
For me to understand,
I still knew what it meant
To hold my Daddy's hand.
When I was much too young
To grasp the preacher's speech,
Yet I could grasp God's love
When Mom would kiss my cheek.
When I at church was asked
How should we love each other?
I knew because back home
I had a crippled brother.

The most important trip a man can make is that involved in meeting the other fellow halfway.
—Brice Van Horn

I TRIED HARD NOT TO SEE

Attempting to leave the Saviour
When skeptic doubts besieged
I found I could not doubt
Though I tried hard to leave.
Excluding God I vowed
That He may not re-enter,
Only to discover He never
Deserted me, a sinner.
Denouncing faith in Christ
I tried hard not to see,
But faith survived because
I knew He died for me.

HOW BLESSINGS COME

I prayed incessantly
That God my heart would bless,
But blessings were withheld
And I prayed less and less.
But I in diligence
Set out to do God's will
And all the joys I'd sought
Became a blessing real.
I seek no blessing now
But I have one request,
"Lord help me do Thy will,"
And doing it I'm blest.

The Lord is at hand.   **Philippians 4:5**

Upright Upbringing

It would be more honorable to our distinguished ancestors to praise them in words less, but in deeds to imitate them more. **Horace Mann**

Good breeding consists in concealing how much we think of ourselves and how little we think of the other person.

HELPING PEOPLE IN THE WRONG WAY

Because I had no time
To teach him how to fish,
I fed the beggar trout
And blue-gill on a dish.
Too tired to share my faith
With him who had a crutch
I shared, instead, some coins
And he thanked me very much.
With ease I urged my child,
"Depend on me alone,"
'Til sheltered years left him
Without a faith his own.

BOYS ARE LIKE CLAY

Boys are this and boys are that
And boys are what you make them,
For they, like clay, set in their mold
And all the world can't break them.
For boys are this and boys are that
And we must never, never
Misguide a boy or mishape one
Deforming him forever.
For boys are this and boys are that
And may we see our duty
To mold them while we have a chance
Into a life of beauty.

GOOD CHILDREN ARE JUST AS LUCKY

Whenever I hear someone
Congratulating parents
"You're lucky to have good children,"
I try to show forbearance.
But silently I find myself thinking
Concerning the much praised youth,
"Indeed those parents are lucky
But don't omit one other truth:
Good children are just as lucky
To have what God oft gives,
Parents, whose children can follow
Examples their parents live."

Since teen-agers are too old to do the things kids do and not old enough to do the things adults do, they do things nobody else does.

THE WISDOM OF A MOTHER

When in his college room
She saw pictures not nice,
She quietly hung by them
A portrait of the Christ.
Days passed and she returned
To find the pictures gone,
Except Christ's portrait there
Which artist's brush had drawn.
She asked, "What happened, Son?"
He cried, "When I saw them
Beside the Christ, I said,
'They just don't go with him.'"

From his youth I reared him as a father, and from his mother's womb I guided him.

Job 31:18

Vice and Virtue

Humanity is never so beautiful as when praying
for forgiveness, or else forgiving another.
Jean Paul Richter

PROBLEMS AT CHURCH

If you should find the perfect church
Without one fault or smear,
For goodness sake! don't join that church;
You'd spoil the atmosphere.
If you should find the perfect church
Where all anxieties cease,
Then pass it by lest joining it
You mar the masterpiece.
If you should find the perfect church
Then don't you ever dare
To tread upon such holy ground;
You'd be a misfit there.
But since no perfect church exists
Made of imperfect men,
Then let's cease looking for that church
And love the church we're in.
Of course it's not a perfect church.
That's simple to discern.
But you and I and all of us
Could cause the tide to turn.
What fools we are to flee our post
In that unfruitful search
To find at last where problems loom
God proudly builds His church.
So let's keep working in our church
Until the resurrection,
And then we each will join God's Church
Without an imperfection.

Be virtuous and you will be happy; but you will
be lonesome, sometimes.   —Edgar W. Nye

His heart was as great as the world, but there
was no room in it to hold the memory of a
wrong.   —Ralph Waldo Emerson

TO FORGIVE IS TO FORGET

I said, "I will forgive
But I can ne'er forget,"
And I heard whispered words
Which I remember yet.
"Did God forgive your sins
And still remember them?"
With shame I dropped my head
As I replied to Him,
"Of course, the Lord forgets
When He forgives, it's true."
"Then go," He said, "Forgive
As I've forgiven you."

PUT-OFF STREET IS SO PLEASANT

There's a certain Mrs. Meant-to
I'd love for you to meet
In the town of Good Intentions.
She lives on Put-off street.
She fills her life with plans
Of good things she will do
For church and school and friends
But all her plans fall through.
I wish she'd leave our town for good
But she won't move away.
Put-off street is so pleasant.
Mrs. Meant-to is here to stay.

The shatterer has come up against you. Man the
ramparts; watch the road; gird your loins; collect
all your strength.   **Nahum 2:1**

Victim or Victor

Victories that are easy are cheap. Those only are worth having which come as the result of hard fighting.   **Henry Ward Beecher**

Life demands from you only the strength you possess. Only one feat is possible—not to have run away.   —Dag Hammerskjold

WHEN DARK NIGHTS HAVE PASSED

When we are all forlorn
God cheers us in the night
By studding blackest skies
With stars of hope and light.
And such display of grace
Becomes to us who grope
A token of God's love
And our lighthouse of hope.
And when dark nights have passed
And morning rises fair,
We'll praise the stars of hope
And God who placed them there.

GOD'S GRACE EXCEEDS MAN'S NEED

If God bestows on you
A burden to be borne,
Then you can count on this:
He'll not leave you forlorn.
For God gives strength to match
Each burden He bestows,
And when your load's increased
His power in you grows.
No matter what life brings
A Christian should not fear it;
The more you're asked to bear,
The more God shares His Spirit.

MIRACLES STILL OCCUR

Like a derelict ship
I drifted on life's sea
Completely unaware
That Jesus cared for me.
And like a wayward cloud
I went with every wind;
Unloved I could not love,
Except myself and sin.
But miracles still occur
For all one hopes to see
Takes place when Christ forgives;
At least it did for me.

THE SCULPTOR

"What is your task?" I plainly asked,
And he gazed long at me
And said with upturned head and eyes,
"Setting an angel free!"
"But I can't see an angel, Sir,"
I answered as I stood,
And he just chipped away and smiled,
"Oh, don't you wish you could?"
Imprisoned in our stony hearts
An angel form resides,
And Jesus ever seeks to carve
His image on our lives.
And when we cannot see a thing
Our Master sees the good,
And says to all who cannot see,
"Oh, don't you wish you could?"

May we shout for joy over your victory, and in the name of our God set up our banners!
Psalms 20:5

Vocational Venture

Great trials seem to be a necessary preparation
for great duties. **Edward Thomson**

I don't know what your destiny will be but one thing I know: the only ones among you who will be really happy are those who will have sought and found how to serve.

—Albert Schweitzer

LASTING VALUES

Go spend your life for values
Which shall outlast your life,
And go invest in treasures
Which shall survive earth's strife.
Get gems you cannot crush,
And gold, time can't consume,
And silver that you'll cherish
When death's bleak shadows loom.
Trusting Christ brings riches,
And doing God's will on earth
Provides, when gold has tarnished,
Treasures of lasting worth.

GAMBLING BIG

Life is a game of chance
And each must take his fling;
The coward ventures not.
The brave risk everything.
Small men hold back their best
Only to learn too late
The great rewards of life
Elude all but the great.
A challenge and a chance
With glory that enhances
Is how life is made up,
And great men take great chances.

OUR WORK IS PLANNED

God has not promised
A task untiring,
A pleasant place
With work inspiring.
God has not promised
A life of ease
Where work delights
And people please.
But God has promised
That every man
Has a task assigned
Like a blue-print plan.
And He has promised
Time is extended
For each to finish
Work God intended.

The vocation of every man and woman is to serve other people. —Leo Tolstoi

WHAT ARE WE HERE FOR

What are we here for?
Not to gather wealth,
Or capture great fame
Or enjoy health.
We're here for one thing
And that's to help each other,
To heal some broken hearts
To lift a fallen brother.
And these are all our brothers
And they are all in need,
And we're here to help them
In words and gifts and deeds.

In all these things we are more than conquerors
through him who loved us. **Romans 8:37**

Willing Worker

Lord, grant that I may always desire more than I can accomplish. **Michelangelo**

It is great to do the Lord's work, but it is greater to do the Lord's will. —Miriam Booth

The more we have to do, the more we are rested, and the less we have to do, the more tired we are. Nothing rests a man so much as plenty to do. —Bishop Quayle

No one is useless in this world who lightens the burden of it for any one else.

—Charles Dickens

WORK IS THE SECRET

If you can work, and not complain
Nor think hard work is e'er in vain
Nor ask too oft, "What do I gain?"
You'll climb the ladder of success.
If you can work, but not forsake
The rules of life which others break,
And strive to keep your mind awake,
You'll climb the ladder of success.
If you can work when others quit
Nor leave unfinished one small bit
When you'd prefer forsaking it,
You'll climb the ladder of success.
If you can work nor count the cost
Of bearing bravely your own cross
And toiling on when all seems lost,
You'll climb the ladder of success.
If you'll work on nor fear to go
The path of tiredness, toil and woe,
Some day at last you'll surely know
You've climbed the ladder of success.

MORE SAINTS NEEDED

I saw a saint today
Though saints are rather rare;
Yet he whom I beheld
Was not engaged in prayer.
Instead he was at work
In common working clothes,
And as he worked he sang
With face and eyes that glowed.
He sang a song of faith
And was to God's grand cause
A channel of His love,
A saint in overalls.

There is nothing so fatal to character as half-finished tasks. —David Lloyd George

WHAT'S WRONG WITH WORK

Low interest rates on money,
So most experts agree,
Is what we most need now
To keep this country free.
But isn't work important?
Would not that bless this age?
Higher interest in work—
Honestly earning one's wage.
America needs foremost,
Before we go berserk,
Not lower interest on money
But greater interest in work.

I never did anything worth doing by accident, nor did any of my inventions come by accident; they came by work. —Thomas Edison

Knowing that whatever good anyone does, he will receive the same again from the Lord.

Ephesians 6:8

116

Winsome Witnessing

*What I want is, not to possess religion, but to have
a religion that shall possess me.*

Charles Kingsley

BUT HE IS WITH US NOW

If Christ came in the flesh
To visit us again
He'd bring no brand new message,
He'd say, "Be born again."
If Christ were to return
Our modern world to tread,
He'd give no fresh command
He'd say what He once said.
If Christ by chance came now
To face our common lot,
He'd come with no new teaching
He'd say, "Trust Me, fear not."
But is He not with us
As sure as long ago?
And does He not still speak
Through Scriptures that we know?
We hear today each time
We read the sacred page
The self-same words of Jesus
As in that ancient age.

The serene, silent beauty of a holy life is the
most powerful influence in the world, next to the
might of the Spirit of God.   —Blaise Pascal

The best manner of avenging ourselves is by not
resembling him who has injured us.

—Jane Porter

WHEN MEN STAND UP

Let strong men stand for Christ
And let wives follow them,
And then their children challenged
Will also stand for Him.
Let strong men stand for Christ
And boys and girls impressed
Will follow in their steps.
They follow men the best.
Let strong men stand for Christ
If we would save our youth
From sensual, selfish paths,
For Christ, the Way and Truth.

WHAT DOES IT TAKE

What does it take to win a soul?
Sometimes you'd be surprised.
Some souls are won by love they see
Expressed in friendly eyes.
What does it take to win a soul?
No effort quite compares
With just one sincere word of praise
Mixed with our silent prayers.
What does it take to win a soul?
For some it just requires
A whispered word mixed with a smile
Conveying Faith's desires.

Orthodoxy of words is blasphemy unless it is
backed up by superiority of character.

—Blaise Pascal

*The Lord is just in all his ways, and kind in all
his doings.*   **Psalms 145:17**

Wonder of Worship

Satan doesn't care what we worship, as long as
we don't worship God.   **Dwight Lyman Moody**

I wish Christianity were more productive of good works, not holy-day keeping, sermon-hearing, or making long prayers, filled with flatteries and compliments despised by wise men, and much less capable of pleasing the Deity.

—Benjamin Franklin

THE BEGINNING OF SERVICE

He came to the church entrance
And whispered to a friend,
"I've come to get my wife;
Has the service come to an end?"
"The worship is nearly over,"
The usher whispered, grinning,
"But the service you speak of
Is just beginning."

THINGS AREN'T AS THEY SEEM

I've learned when God seems far removed
He's really very close;
God hides Himself to test our faith
Just when we need Him most.
It's when He seems so far away
He's closer to us then,
(At least we learn it later on)
Than He has ever been.
Lord, help us learn faith's lesson well
That things aren't as they seem;
You're nearest when You seem withdrawn
And closer than we dream.

EXPERIENCE

I accept the law of gravity
And other scientific concepts
Of Newton, Faraday, and others
Concerning falling objects.
But most of all I believe
Because I've fallen myself;
I've experienced the law of gravity;
And I'm forced to accept.
That's why I accept the Bible,
A hell to shun, a heaven above;
I believe, because I've experienced
God's Presence, His power, His love.

TAKE TIME TO PRAY

I'm sure we are not heard
For lengthy prayers we pray,
And yet in praying much
Our faith grows every day.
And it's a well known fact
That those who tarry long
Rise from their secret place
With faith and courage strong.
And if we took the time
To tarry long in prayer
Our faith would grow and grow
While we were kneeling there.

Christianity is not a puzzle to be solved, but a way of life to be adopted. It is not a creed to be memorized but a person to follow.

Guard your steps when you go to the house of
God; to draw near to listen is better than to offer
the sacrifice of fools.   **Ecclesiastes 5:1**

Wonderful Women

That the woman was made of a rib out of the side of Adam; not out of his feet to be trampled upon by him, but out of his side to be equal with him, under his arm to be protected, and near his heart to be loved. **Matthew Henry**

A perfect husband is one who stands by his wife in troubles she wouldn't have, had she not married.

A LETTER TO MOTHER

On this another Mother's Day,
Mother, I am so far away
That of all things I wish you knew
My thoughts today are thoughts of you.
What joy to think of memories sweet,
Of bygone years when at your feet
I propped my head upon your knees
And learned to pray those childish pleas.
And though today I'm far from you
I pray that selfsame prayer I knew,
"Now I lay me down to sleep,"
'Til rude awareness makes me weep
That I'm not all I planned to be
When once I knelt beside your knee.
But Mother dear, if you'll forgive
And if henceforth God lets me live
I'll prove the prayers I've heard you pray
Were answered on this Mother's Day.

I'm not denying that women are foolish; God Almighty made 'em to match the men.
—George Eliot

I GIVE THEE A RING

I give to thee a ring
And place it on thy hand,
A symbol of my love
That's endless like this band.
I give to thee a ring
That means so much to me
For gold has always been
A gift for royalty.
I give to thee a gift,
A perfect-circled ring,
And its perfection tells
My love's a perfect thing.
I give to thee a ring
Betokening in part
The grander gift bestowed
When I gave you my heart.

SHE WANTS TO HEAR

If you are fortunate
To have a loving wife,
You ought to pay her back
Though it takes all your life.
Those generous words of praise
And sharing every load
Are thoughtfulness you owe
As you walk down life's road.
And since she means so much
Why not make her aware
That you are still in love
And that you really care.

A woman who fears the Lord is to be praised.
Proverbs 31:30

Worry Is Wrong

Talk to Him in prayer of all your wants, your troubles, even of the weariness you feel in serving Him. **Francis de S. Fenelon**

Hope for the best, get ready for the worst; take cheerfully what God chooses to send.

WORRY IS A SIN

Of all sins Jesus scorned
Not one was ever mentioned
With quite the scorn he felt
For fear and apprehension.
For Jesus said to those
Rushed with fear and life's hurries,
"Have no anxiety
About tomorrow's worries."
For worry is a thief
That defrauds every day
Our souls of inner peace
As we go on our way.
Christ called a spade a spade
And He called worry sin,
The badge of unbelief,
The sign of doubting men.

YOU KNOW THESE

There are two souls indeed
The world can do without;
One is old "Used-to-be,"
The other is "I-doubt."
And while old "Used-to-be"
Dreams of the days gone by,
"I-doubt" fears days ahead
And whines, "I dare not try."
Old "Used-to-be" looks back
Stupid and satisfied;
"I-doubt" won't even try;
Fear has him paralyzed.

WHEN FAITH COMES BACK

Anxiety walked with me,
And faith I long denied
Came back to prove its worth
And walked close by my side.
And my anxieties
Soon felt the magic spell
Which faith so freely cast
When faith came back to dwell.
Of course, anxiety fled
And I, released, went free,
Grateful indeed that faith
Came back to walk with me.

TEARS BLIND OUR EYES

"Why weepest thou?" The Master asked
Of Mary Magdalene,
And He today asks us the same
Amidst life's tearful scenes.
For we like her, bowed low with grief,
And fearful of tomorrow,
See not the Master standing near,
Tears blind our eyes with sorrow.
Yet still He asks, "Why weepest Thou?"
And in our troubled years
He comes to us in love and asks
The meaning of our tears.
And when He comes He speaks to us,
Bowed low in unbelief,
He speaks great words of faith and love
Interpreting our grief.

If God is for us, who is against us?

Romans 8:31

or God alone my soul waits in silence.   **Psalms 62:5**

SILENT THINGS

Let me remember silent things,
Remembered from my childhood springs;
Slow melting snow on sun-splashed peaks,
Mute trees that try with buds to speak,
And spring-time sun that gently goes
As silent as it first arose.
Let me remember silent things
Like winter's rosy fireside scenes,
And snow, fresh-fallen, soft and deep
That charmed us 'til we fell asleep,
And silent trees all caked with snow
Like saints at prayer with heads bowed low.
If I recall these silent things
It matters not what my life brings.
In woe I'm sure I'll stand steadfast
And win my cherished goal at last,
To be an isle of peace and poise,
Amidst life's sea of strife and noise.

A time to keep silence, and a time to speak.
Ecclesiastes 3:7

You and Yuletide

It is good to be children sometimes, and never better than at Christmas, when its mighty Founder was a child Himself.   **Charles Dickens**

EVERYBODY NEEDS A STAR

The wise of every age
Have found it's not too far
To go to Bethlehem
If guided by a star.
Nor is the way too long
Nor journey too high priced
If such a pilgrimage
Results in finding Christ.
For some the Church becomes
A light that leads them far;
For me a Christ-like friend
Became my guiding star.

THE PICTURE AND THE PERSON

Men on tiptoes of faith
Oft glimpsed God from afar
And wrote it in a Book
For sinners as we are.
And when men read of it
They had their spirits stirred,
Though word-portraits all seemed
Off-focus and half-blurred.
Word-pictures helped men's faith
But when on earth Christ trod,
No portrait was required;
Men saw the face of God.

The earth has grown old with its burden of care
but at Christmas the world is young again.

THE FIRST CHRISTMAS

When earth was black as night
With no prospect of morn
God said, "Let there be light!"
And lo, the Christ was born.
When Herod ruled as if
Men's souls weren't worth a thing
God said, "I'll save my world,"
And He sent forth a King.
When men were slaves and serfs
All tortured with their pains,
God said, "I'll set men free,"
And Christ came breaking chains.
When infants were despised
And children were forlorn
God said, "I'll be a child,"
And it was Christmas morn.

HE COMES DISGUISED

I think God knew how much
His visit here would please us,
But He disguised Himself
And came to earth as Jesus.
We'd planned for Him to come
A splendor-laden King,
But He disguised Himself
And came a baby-thing.
God, still disguised, draws near
And so each Christmas charms
As much as when He came
Disguised in Mary's arms.

Be not afraid; for behold, I bring you good news of a great joy which will come to all the people; for to you is born this day in the city of David a Savior, who is Christ the Lord.   **Luke 2:10–11**

Youth Years

Youth, when thought is speech and speech is truth. **Walter Scott**

FOR LOVE OF BEAUTY

From piles of stone and lumber,
Two brothers took some boards
And built on lots adjoining
The best they could afford.
One brother built with skill
And a lot of planning
From the lumber provided
An elegant mansion.
The other built a hovel
Out of identical material
Because he lacked a plan
And had no building skill.
In life we're character-building
And oft from gifts the same,
One builds for love of beauty—
Another builds to shame.

WHEN YOU MEET THAT GIRL

Young man, God has reserved
A girl sincere and true,
The girl of all your dreams
And God plans her for you.
And you can count on this
That God will guide you to her
If you will do God's will
Becoming braver, truer.
And when you meet that girl,
Young man, you will rejoice
That you kept yourself pure,
Worthy of God's first choice.

When there is really a tough job to be done, get an experienced person. When there's an impossible task, only a young person will do.

CREED FOR YOUTH

Go venture life upon a dream,
Reach for the stars, follow the gleam;
Cling to your hopes by faith's surmise.
Walk with your head high in the skies.
And don't forget to venture all
When courage beckons and duty calls.
And give to life all you possess
When it requires your very best.
For soon you'll learn that he who lives
Is only he who truly gives
Of self and love and sacrifice,
That's why it pays to follow Christ.

Don't laugh at a youth for his affectations; he is only trying on one face after another to find his own.
—Logan Pearsall Smith

RETRIBUTION

I said to myself
"My wild oats I'll scatter;
It's nobody's business
My deeds don't matter."
For every thrill I had
A hundred tears I weep;
Each seed of sin I sowed,
A hundred-fold I reap.

Better is a poor and wise youth than an old and foolish king. **Ecclesiastes 7:13**

Youthful Yearnings

**By abstaining from most things it is surprising
how many things we enjoy.   William G. Simms**

My conscience doesn't keep me from doing certain things. It does keep me from enjoying them.

IT'S AS WE WILL IT

The wise man's fame had spread afar
For all who questioned him,
Went forth, indeed, inspired because
Of how he answered them.
A skeptic came to prove the man
Was not as wise as that;
He caught a bird and brought it to
The place the wise man sat.
"Wise man, tell me," the youth inquired
Of him so blind and old;
"Is this bird alive or dead, which I
Within my hands now hold?"
The man saw through the scheme for if
He said the bird was dead,
The youth would let it fly away
Disproving what he said.
If he declared it was alive,
The youth with hands so strong
Would crush the bird and then proclaim
The wise man's words were wrong.
"It's up to you! my lad," he said
With caution's gentle spirit;
"That bird is like the life we live,
It's always as we will it!"

Before our conscience punishes us as a judge,
it warns us as a friend.

THE FARMER'S SON

They went to see him graduate
For he had passed the test,
And they were thrilled he'd won the prize
For highest grades and best.
Their honored son led from the stage
His classmates with a smile,
And passing by his parents' row
He paused right in the aisle.
He kissed her cheeks and pinned on her
The medal he had won,
And then he said, "Daddy, I owe
A lot to you and Mom."
The farmer said with low-bowed head,
"Best crop I can recall."
And she with tears of joy replied,
"It's sure been worth it all."

THE GOLDEN RULE

Be such a man today
And then live such a life
That if all followed you
True peace would cancel strife.
And do to others here
Not as they always do,
But act as you would like
For all to act toward you.
So act if it became
A universal act
Earth would become, indeed,
A paradise, in fact.

**The fear of the Lord is the beginning of knowledge; fools despise wisdom and instruction.
Proverbs 1:7**

Zeal and Zest

Some people are always grumbling because roses have thorns. I am thankful that thorns have roses.
Alphonse Karr

An optimist laughs to forget; a pessimist forgets to laugh.

A PLACE FOR STARTING OVER

One thing above all things
I wish that I could find,
A place for starting over—
The land of being kind.
A cross to crucify
My spirit too demanding,
A spot to leave behind
Each harsh misunderstanding,
That I might start anew,
And yet each dawn, somehow,
I hear my Master whispering,
"The time and place is now."

God loves a cheerful doer as well as a cheerful giver.

YOU'RE ON YOUR OWN

When tiny birds are hatched
They're nourished in the nest
Until the mother gives
Each fledgling bird the test.
For when at last she's sure
Each half-grown bird can fly
She shoves it from the nest
And forces it to try.
So life is much like that
And happy is the man
Who when he first takes wing
Exults, "I can! I can!"

JOY LIKE JESUS HAD

Amidst a feverish world
Gripped with war's hate and madness,
We should exemplify
A life of joy and gladness.
A life un-counterfeit
And by such joy possessed
That we may each become
The love of God expressed.
For all the world is tired
Of faith that makes men sad;
Grant gladness to us, God,
And joy like Jesus had.

I PROCEED WITH JOY

When I could not go on
Or bear my burdens longer,
Christ stooped to share my load
And made my shoulders stronger.
My trudging feet He touched
Until like feathers light,
I skipped for joy and danced
Along a pathway bright.
His touching me transformed
My cross to silver wings
And I, no longer lonely,
Proceed with joy Christ brings.

An optimist is a fellow who takes the cold water thrown on his idea, heats it with enthusiasm, makes steam and pushes ahead.

Never flag in zeal, be aglow with the Spirit, serve the Lord.
Romans 12:11

Zenith

The highest reward for man's toil is not what he gets for it, but what he becomes by it.

John Ruskin

GETTING THROUGH THE VALLEY

When brighter days shine on my heart
As they will surely do,
And when dark clouds of woe shall rift
To let God's face shine through,
I'll not forget the lessons learned
When I could hardly see;
'Twas then I learned by faith to cling
To Him who walked with me.
When better days have dawned and I'm
No longer tempest torn,
And sorrow's night recedes as joy
Comes trailing down the morn,
I'll then recall that sorrow taught
Sweet truths I had not known,
And tears became my telescope
Through which I viewed God's throne.

BRIDGE BUILDING

If I my world could choose
I'd ask the all-wise Giver
To let me build a bridge
Across some angry river.
Or else tear down some wall
Where neighbors used to walk,
And then I'd clear a path
So they could meet and talk.
For that's the greatest work
And that is why I'd rather
Blast walls and build bridges,
So friends could get together.

CLEANSED FROM CONVICTION

If you should seek sincerely
To know the Saviour dear,
You'll learn to love Him dearly
And find Him very near.
If you with heart condemned
Seek Christ, the friend of sinners,
You will with ease find Him
Anxious your life to enter.
If you with broken heart
Should seek the Lord believing,
He will impart most gladly
His solace for your grieving.
If you quite conscience-stricken
Should ask Christ to forgive,
You'll find, cleansed from conviction,
Yourself prepared to live.

WHEN STORMS ASSAIL

When everything goes wrong
And I'm a bit discouraged,
I always pray this prayer,
"Lord, send me extra courage."
When closest friends forsake
And I in darkness sit,
I always pray this prayer,
"Lord, please don't let me quit."
When storms of life assail
And I, forlorn, have sorrowed,
I shout above the storm,
"Lord, please help me go forward."

Seek the things that are above, where Christ is, seated at the right hand of God.

Colossians 3:1

isdom is with the aged, and understanding in length of days.
Job 12:12

LET'S USE YESTERYEARS

The past unchanged remains
In spite of all regret,
And tears we shed in shame
Cannot make us forget.
But we can make of failure
A stepping stone to duty,
And turn remorse into
Stairways that lead to beauty.
Then let's use yesteryears
With all its dread and terrors
As a ladder of success
From failure's foolish errors.

They still bring forth fruit in old age, they are
ever full of sap and green.   **Psalms 92:14**